Hamden

Hamden

Tales from the Sleeping Giant

ERIC D. LEHMAN

Charleston · London

THE
History
PRESS

Published by The History Press
Charleston, SC 29403
www.historypress.net

First published 2010

Manufactured in the United States

ISBN 978.1.59629.835.4

Lehman, Eric D.
Hamden : tales from the Sleeping Giant / Eric D. Lehman.
p. cm.
Includes bibliographical references.
ISBN 978-1-59629-835-4
1. Hamden (Conn.)--History--Anecdotes. 2. Hamden (Conn.)--Social life and customs-
-Anecdotes. 3. Hamden (Conn.)--Intellectual life--Anecdotes. 4. Community life--
Connecticut--Hamden--History--Anecdotes. 5. Hamden (Conn.)--Biography--Anecdotes.
I. Title.
F104.H2L44 2010
974.6'7--dc22
2010006753

Then up above Mount Carmel's towering crest,
We saw the autumn foliage and the pines,
And far away upon the Giant's breast,
We studied out his form in curving lines.

A Sleeping Giant! lying there in state,
His head is pillowed on a running stream,
And laves his temples, while night's shadows wait,
But noon still finds him in his quiet dream…

Through all the wild scenes of his deep seclusion
And changing shadows of his dim retreat,
My fancy, with a touch of strange delusion,
Would bring him quickly on his Giant feet.

—from "Legend of the Sleeping Giant" by Charles Merriman, 1887

Contents

Prologue

I magine a typical family traveling on the scenic Wilbur Cross Parkway in the late twentieth century, tunneling through the cliff wall of West Rock and cruising down the Hamden offramp. This road-tripping clan might have been planning on a nostalgic trip to one of the first outdoor strip malls in the United States. They could have been heading toward the golden arches of the first McDonalds in Connecticut. Or they may have been on their way up Whitney Avenue to hike the green crests of the Sleeping Giant. But what awaited them just off the exit on the "magic mile" was a strange, nearly apocalyptic sight: a silhouetted row of cars half buried in asphalt along Route 10.

The owner of the Hamden Plaza had commissioned this unusual work from Site, an eclectic group of artists known for similar installations, but this Ghost Parking Lot would be a masterpiece. Framing the entrance to the ordinary parking lot, separated by traditional white lines, these drowned vehicles rose and fell like a wave of automotive sea. The unusual, perhaps shocking sculpture tempted visitors to walk by it, around it, through it. The travelers may have noted the familiar curve of a Volkswagen Beetle or compared the family station wagon to one trapped in macadam. As they toured the concrete walkway that fronted the stores, they would have found wind sculptures and interactive displays by modern masters like James Seawright, Maura Sheehan and George Rhoads. A day of shopping turned into a day spent in an art gallery.

Back in 1955, when this open-air mall was first built on the site of Henry Peters's orchard, it heralded the new age of suburban expansion, and now it trumpeted the future again. A plaque told interested viewers that the Ghost Parking Lot's purpose was to combine two elements of a shopping center

The Ghost Parking Lot at Hamden Plaza was one of the first "site-specific" works of art in America. *Courtesy of the Hamden Arts Commission.*

in an astonishing way and give spectators "another frame of reference." It was supposed to "generate dialogue in the community," and it certainly did. Some loved this ambitious effort to make art more public, and some derided it as a stunt or an eyesore. What were these buried automobiles supposed to mean? Were they supposed to be archaeological relics of a former age? Did they look toward a future beyond suburbia? The ambiguous exhibit may never have sparked agreement from visitors or locals, but it did appear in hundreds of art books.

Those who knew Hamden, Connecticut, might have expected such innovation and originality. This was an area that had grown from a small colonial settlement into a thriving town, blending five village centers into an organic whole. Often called the "bedroom of New Haven," the rambling, multitiered suburb was more truly a studio, where pioneers and dreamers lived intense lives amidst calm green hills. By the time the Ghost Parking Lot shrugged up from the earth like a futuristic symbol, Hamden already hosted authors, sculptors and architects. Inventors like Eli Whitney and A.C. Gilbert forged the town with their unceasing commitment to creation, while the community banded together to save the mighty Sleeping Giant.

That family who rumbled off the Wilbur Cross Parkway could have seen themselves mirrored in one of the town's famous families, like the Dickermans or the Wilders. Perhaps they found inspiration in Hamden's books, buildings or stories. They surely wanted to explore why this exquisite river valley enfolded in high trap rock ridges seemed to nurture the spirits of these talented men and women. And at the end of the day, they would have discovered that whether you visited Hamden or called it home, this was a place that could shape the landscapes of imagination.

CHAPTER I

A Place for Revolution

As Matthew Gilbert sailed into New Haven Harbor in 1638, he must have seen the giant supine form in the northern distance, its pine-covered flanks blue against the April sky. He and the five hundred other Puritan settlers arrived to found a new colony, and as one of the first off the ship, Gilbert fell to his knees in gratitude. He was joined by people like William Bradley, who served as captain in Oliver Cromwell's army and settled in the colony to avoid the tyranny of a monarchical system. They would be the "founders of the theocracy," an ideal Puritan state that hoped to right the wrongs of the old world. To do this, the settlers kept a careful balance between the rights of the individual and the needs of the community. Property sales had to be approved, and resources like timber had to be watched closely. This early ideal inspired families like the Gilberts and the Bradleys, and they saw civic duty as a vital part of human life.

The river valley and surrounding hills settled by Matthew Gilbert and the Puritans were previously the territory of natives known as the Quinnipiac, meaning "long water land." By the time of this encounter, the natives had been devastated by European plagues for over one hundred years, including recent epidemics in 1633 and 1634. The once numerous people were too weak to challenge the relatively few New Haven colonists and struck a treaty with Governor Eaton. As far as the Quinnipiac were concerned, the new settlers were no worse than the powerful Mohawks who had previously demanded tribute.

Taller than the English settlers, the Quinnipiac wore buckskins and bear fur. In the summer, they dressed in breechcloths and skirts, and in the winter they added leather leggings, aprons and cloaks. They dwelt in domed wigwams covered with mats of bark and rushes. They paddled up and down the rivers in search of trout and turtles in twenty-foot canoes made by hollowing logs with fire and scraping them clean with stones. The hills north of the Quinnipiac villages were prime hunting grounds, and for centuries they had walked their secret paths in search of fox and deer. Now they joined the settlers, fighting as scouts in King Philip's War. The young braves saw the opportunity for positive action, and for the next hundred years the Quinnipiac chose to join the English wars in the West Indies, Cuba and Canada. Many also died of diseases, and the tribe slowly declined.

Trapping beaver was the first English industry in the Quinnipiac hunting grounds north of New Haven. The area was quickly trapped out, and interest waned, except for in a flat stretch of earth directly northwest of New Haven. However, some colonists saw a different use for the rivers once dammed by beavers. A mill sprang up along the west branch, where the main path of the Quinnipiac Indians crossed the river at a rocky ledge under the tall monolith of East Rock. Despite a lack of success over decades of early colonization, this site gave its utilitarian name to the river. Then, in 1661, it became a shelter for two of the infamous regicides, Edward Whalley and William Goffe. Pursued by agents of the British Crown for their crime, they fled again to a jumble of boulders at the top of West Rock, the other sentinel that framed the Mill River Valley. Between these two rocky hills, slow immigration took place, though it mostly involved the cows and horses of absentee owners. Only shepherd Nehemiah Smith lived farther out than this, grazing his sheep in the wolf-haunted dales.

In March 1663, Matthew Gilbert cleared a swath of wild country at the junction of Shepard's Brook and the Mill River, needing space to raise horses and hay. A year after landing, Gilbert had been chosen as the earliest deacon of the first church. Later, he married Jane Baker, became a magistrate and emerged as second in civil affairs to Governor Eaton. This was formalized when he was elected the first deputy governor of the colony. So now Gilbert's prominence in the community drew the colony's attention to the long river valley and high hills. Four years later, people started mining high-grade clay along the rivers and brooks, and a few brave farmers hacked into the wilderness.

By 1704, Matthew Gilbert's land had been divided among his sons, and his grandson Daniel would settle permanently at Centerville. Others had moved from the plains into the hills. But the rocky area between Gilbert's farm and the Cheshire community ten miles north was slow to be occupied.

The Mill River became a lifeline through the hills of Hamden. *Courtesy of Magnus Wahlstrom Library, University of Bridgeport.*

Hunters and shepherds knew these trap rock ridges but did not build there. In 1720, a few farming families like Peck, Warner and Cooper settled in this wild territory. In 1729, Daniel Bradley, great-grandson of William, built a sawmill on West Todd to grind flour.

This small mill may have encouraged Joel Munson to build a dam across the Mill River in the shadow of the Sleeping Giant, sometimes called Mount Carmel. This wild land was about to be civilized. Munson set up a large operation to grind corn and saw wood, encouraging settlers to farm farther north, away from the protected peninsula of New Haven. New paths and roads converged at this point from west, north, east and south. Other mills sprang up along the brooks and rills west of the Cheshire Road. The Ives and Dickerman families cleared land in 1740. Then Samuel Bellamy, whose father was an innkeeper in Cheshire, opened his tavern in 1743. His wife, Mary Jones, ran the kitchen and planted lilacs in the yard. Soon, ox teams trundling south toward New Haven found the perfect watering hole and evening rest. The next morning they could make it to the market and back to the tavern by dusk for a second night at Bellamy's Tavern.

With a mill and tavern, this was now a village. More sawmills were built, such as Waite Chatterton's in 1750. Each family was completely self-reliant, growing flax, spinning and weaving cloth and often forging their own tools.

Although this photo of Mount Carmel shows the Lower Axle Shop during the nineteenth century, the building contained remnants of Munson's Mill. *Courtesy of the Hamden Historical Society.*

A trap rock formation called "the Steps" hampered travel in the area, so Joel Munson carved a suitable cart road over it. In 1760, bridges were built across the streams that fed the Mill River. Tin peddlers came over these rough roads and bridges to barter with the farmers' wives. For entertainment, men tried to beat the brawny Doolittle family at trials of strength, which included lifting four-hundred-pound beams and full cider barrels. Some of the more witty citizens banded together in an early lampoon society called Dog Lane Court. The man elected "judge" of this court had to get away with telling the biggest lie, and offenders were often crowned with a turtle shell as punishment.

More serious things were also afoot. Samuel Bellamy, Daniel Bradley, Waite Chatterton and Joel Munson petitioned the colony to form a Congregational church in 1757. Ezra Stiles came to the church to preach. A new church meant a new parish because the two ideas were inseparable at the time. In 1758, the farmers began discussing parish business in the tavern and set about building a proper meetinghouse for Mount Carmel. The gristmills in the hills prospered, handed down to the next generation of settlers. More planters broke ground around the old Gilbert farm area, building houses close to the new roads that angled in from New Haven.

At the time of the Continental Congress, a committee of inspection was formed in New Haven to oversee war matters, and Samuel Atwater and Jonathan Dickerman of Hamden served on it. Dickerman was chosen as grand juror in 1776. Men from Mount Carmel continued to serve on these Revolutionary committees throughout the war, proving the parish's interest in the cause of independence. One of these men was John Gilbert, great-grandson of Matthew. John was also instrumental in the formation of the Seventeenth Company of minutemen from North Haven and Mount Carmel, in case of emergency. In 1778, he snuck five bushels of rare, handmade salt to rebels in the British-controlled New York City. His second lieutenant in the company was none other than Joel Bradley, great-great-grandson of William, who had landed with Matthew Gilbert generations earlier.

Three years after the signing of the Declaration of Independence, New Haven readied itself to celebrate its anniversary. It fell on a Sunday, so Monday the fifth was scheduled for the intricate, patriotic ceremonies. However, in the middle of the night warning guns went off, and by dawn, President Ezra Stiles of Yale College spotted the British ships with his telescope. Thousands of soldiers under General Tryon landed in West Haven and marched for the city. Many citizens fled north to East Rock and the Sleeping Giant. Stiles sent his daughters off to Mount Carmel, along with valuable Yale records.

But not everyone went north. Those able-bodied minutemen of the Mill River Valley marched south to fight the invaders with their old "Queen's arms," muskets that had probably only been used on squirrels and rabbits. Meanwhile, the New Haven volunteers met the British at the West Bridge and, despite taking casualties, drove them back. Instead of pushing their luck at the bridge, the redcoats marched about nine miles to the Derby Road. They were slowed by a small group of American militia, which included James and Timothy Bassett of Hamden, home on furlough from the Continental army. By the time they entered New Haven, Captain Gilbert, Joel Bradley and other men from Hamden arrived and pressed the enemy, while the original force fought a slow retreat into town.

Where Broadway met the Cheshire and Derby roads, at a place called "Ditch Corner," the British released a round of grapeshot, killing many of the American militia. John Gilbert was wounded in the leg and could not retreat fast enough as he vainly tried to reach his horse tied up near the college. His brother Michael and friends from Hamden stuck with him until the British Captain Parker overtook them. Gilbert offered parley and asked if his life would be spared, but Parker refused, calling him a "damned rebel." Knowing that they would be shot, Gilbert said, "We'll never surrender!" and ordered his men to fire at the British officer, killing him. The overwhelming British force fired a round of grapeshot to kill the Hamden volunteers: John and Michael Gilbert, Samuel and Silas Woodin, Joseph Dorman and Asa Todd. A musket ball slammed into James Bassett's arm and broke it. He was dragged from the fray, but not before seeing his brother, Timothy, receive a seemingly mortal wound through the body. A redcoat stole Timothy's silver shoe buckles and raised his weapon to dash out the Hamden man's brains. But the local Tory scout said, "This man has his death wound, let him alone. I have hunted foxes with him many a time." Both wounded Bassetts would miraculously recover.

Captain John Gilbert was not so lucky. His skull was broken by the butt of a rifle and his body stabbed by bayonets. But they could not break the independent spirit of this "gentleman of reputation, beloved and esteemed in life, and lamented in death, who fell in defense of his country." Dozens of other rebels also lost their lives that day, but none died in vain. Finding resistance throughout the city too stiff, the British decided that their force was too small to hold the scrappy colony. They had planned to burn the entire city, but the numbers of militiamen who had arrived daunted the British general, who retreated to his ships. The New Haven soldiers celebrated by drinking twenty gallons of rum.

Men from the territory north of the city served their new country with pride throughout the war. Captain Jonathan Mix marched to Lexington and, as a captain of marines, served in some of the first engagements of the United States navy. Samuel Atwater and Benjamin Warner also marched to Lexington in 1774, among the first to answer the call to revolution. Theophilus Goodyear fought in the Battles of Long Island and White Plains. And at the end of the war, Jonathan Dickerman rode down to New Haven from his house at the base of the Sleeping Giant to sit on the council of 1784 to decide the fate of British Loyalists and supporters. He served on the committee with Pierpont Edwards, later a member of the Continental Congress that ratified the Constitution. They were magnanimous and generous in their admittance of all such people into the new nation, stating:

> *Although at the present moment, while the distress and calamities of the late war are fresh in our recollection, we may consider a persecuting spirit as justifiable, we must, when reason assumed her empire, reproach such a line*

of conduct, and be convinced that future generations, not being influenced by our passions, will form their ideas of our character from those acts.

Hopefully, the reluctant new citizens learned the ways of the United States from men like Timothy Bassett and Joel Bradley, who lived to tell tales of courage to their children.

After the war, the citizens of Mount Carmel continued to meet at the tables of Bellamy's Tavern, now a center of social life. The elder Samuel Bellamy had died young in 1760, the first adult buried at Mount Carmel's official cemetery. Bellamy's son, also named Samuel, did not have to go far to school, since classes were held in his family's tavern. By the Revolution, he had married Hannah Bradley, bought a six-hundred-foot deep copper mine on the Sleeping Giant and taken his own place in town affairs. He drilled militia in the tavern yard and opened a store next to the tavern. His ale barrels were always full, and the people of the parish loved him. One wrote "Colonel Bellamy's March," which takes its place in collections of early patriotic songs alongside "Yankee Doodle."

Bellamy was joined at the inn by other parish worthies, including Amasa Bradley, son of Captain Gilbert's second lieutenant, Joel, and great-great-great-grandson of William. Bradley owned one of Mount Carmel's many sawmills and married Martha Gilbert, joining the two families. He met at the tavern with Bellamy and the others to discuss the founding of a new town. They were farmers, geographically isolated, with different interests from the merchants of New Haven, and they needed a separate government. For their part, New Haven seemed willing to separate, due to the expense of keeping up bridges in the river valley. Though some wanted to keep the name Mount Carmel, it seemed insufficient, since the territory was much larger. Amasa Bradley had another idea.

Amasa's ancestor William had been in Oliver Cromwell's army with John Hampden, and though the Puritan revolutionary had been dead for 143 years, his character was still revered and remembered. Philosopher David Hume had scorned Cromwell as a dictator, but he praised Hampden for his "spirit and courage" and for his "bold stand which he made in defense of the laws and liberties of his country." Hampden had almost escaped the pursuing monarchists and had actually been on board a ship to Connecticut when he was captured. Perhaps Bradley thought he could bring Hampden's spirit to this new world instead.

In 1786, the Connecticut General Assembly granted Hamden, with a silent and later absent *p*, its independence. The new town included all of the

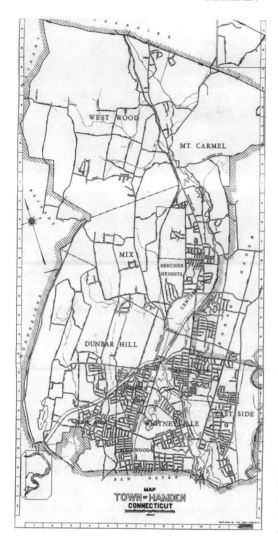

Hamden's diverse villages, from Mount Carmel in the north to Whitneyville in the south, were both a benefit and a challenge for the growing town. *Courtesy of the Hamden Historical Society.*

original Mount Carmel Parish and the East Plains Society lands for three miles south of the intersection of Shepard's Brook, just past the original mill at East Rock. Colonial parish rules became the civil ordinances of a town that had little in common with the wilderness hunted a century and a half before by the Quinnipiac, of whom less than a dozen remained. The rest had migrated to Farmington, absorbed into the Tunxis tribe, though individual wigwams continued to be seen into the early 1800s, and itinerant Indians occasionally wandered through on their ancient, secret paths. The modern road from New Haven to Cheshire now traveled straight and level, a full one hundred feet wide. Timbered houses built on solid red sandstone foundations stood proudly along its length, cornfields filled neighboring valleys and wolves no longer howled from the hills.

Generations of pioneer families had sacrificed to make this home for themselves, through war and toil, gallant acts and simple works. As Hamden author John Dickerman said in later years, "Were they not all heroes who stood shoulder to shoulder for one another? The wilderness had no terrors for them, or if there were terrors they conquered them, but had no time to put their deeds on record." One of those quiet people was Amasa Bradley, who served nine terms as state representative of this new town, carrying forward the ideal of civic duties that the founders of New Haven Colony had championed. But the Bradleys, Bellamys and Gilberts of the past would soon be joined by pioneers of the future who would work in new ways to make the community strong. Now an independent town in an independent nation, Hamden was ready for the revolutions to come.

CHAPTER 2

The Armaments of the Future

By the time Eli Whitney built his legendary Hamden factory in 1798, he was already famous. Born the eldest child of a farming family in Westborough, Massachusetts, in 1765, he set about learning everything he could. When Whitney was twelve, his sister Elizabeth claimed that he had "more general knowledge than men considered of the first standing in the country." He also possessed astonishing dexterity. In his father's workshop, he fashioned wheels and chairs with a lathe, took apart and put back together a pocket watch and made an exact replica of a broken knife blade. At age twelve he fashioned a violin. When he was barely a teenager, Whitney saw a business opportunity in the Revolution, and he installed a forge in his workshop to craft nails. He even hired his first employee.

In 1789, at age twenty-three, he set off for Yale and was admitted personally by the famous president Ezra Stiles. Whitney studied incredible machines in the museum and dreamed of making his own. Little did he know that a tutoring position in South Carolina would offer him that chance. Upon arrival there, he found that the teaching job was not what he had hoped, and furthermore, he contracted a minor case of smallpox. But during these struggles he was inspired when he saw a cat trying to pull a chicken through a fence, ending up with only feathers. Why not use the same process to seed cotton? Six months after his arrival, he built a working model of his "cotton engine."

Whitney set about marketing the device. However, a series of business errors led to problems with the southern planters. Though some honorable farmers bought the "gin" directly from him, many pirated it, dashing his dreams of wealth and crushing his naïve views on the sacred rights of property. He tried to patent the device with Secretary of State Thomas Jefferson, but the courts delayed and refused Whitney's lawsuits. Many people in the South denied that Whitney had even invented the gin. Retreating to New Haven, he wrote bitterly, "The difficulties with which I have had to contend have originated principally in the want of a disposition in Mankind to do justice."

Who knows how this young inventor found the strength to start anew? But somehow he did, and he jumped at the chance when the government issued contracts for ten thousand muskets for a possible war with either France or Britain. Whitney had never manufactured a gun but gamely signed a contract in 1798, guaranteeing the delivery of ten to fifteen thousand muskets two years later. This was a ridiculous number, and others who signed the contracts could produce only an average of one thousand each. But Whitney had the idea to use an interchangeable system, allowing any gun part to match any other. Others had used this system for textiles and basic tools. However, the lock of the musket required precise dimensions. Could he turn the art of extremely skilled craftsmen into a mechanical process? No one had ever tried.

He decided not to try to do this experimental work in New Haven and instead looked northward, up the Cheshire Road, to the new town of Hamden. At the turn of the nineteenth century, most people only used this road to herd oxen, pigs and sheep into market in New Haven. However, there was the ancient mill site on the river between East Rock and Mill Rock, already over 150 years old. It remained the ideal spot—in winter sheltered from strong winds by the hills and in summer cooled off by the trees and river. Water power was obviously available to run machines, and the lower Mill River could be navigated by barge from the harbor to the factory. Whitney's searching mind must have seen the possibilities of the location immediately.

The idyllic spot may have encouraged Whitney to sign the federal contract. The government gave him the black walnut stocks and a $5,000 advance, followed by two more installments later in the process. It was a daunting risk. Though others around the world, and even in New England, were attempting similar feats of speed and efficiency, no communication existed between them. In addition, Whitney was in fact starting the entire project with no means to do so. Only after signing the contract did he buy the land in Hamden and begin recruiting people to help him. He knocked down the old corn mill, laid new foundations and struggled to get the factory built, "worne out with fatigue and anxiety." The first building was seventy-two feet long, thirty feet wide and two stories high. He hired every available workman in the county and built a boardinghouse for unmarried employees.

Eli Whitney's combination of mass production, machine tools and specialized division of labor led to the Industrial Revolution. *Courtesy of Magnus Wahlstrom Library, University of Bridgeport.*

Southern Hamden would become one of the first boomtowns in America.

It soon became clear that Whitney had underestimated the scope of his task: "I find that my personal attention is more constantly and essentially necessary to every branch of the work than I apprehended." He worked sixteen hours a day, dealing with problems as varied as river flooding and import tariffs. Luckily, the challenge of getting unusual and expensive materials was just about to get easier for the inventor. He told a friend:

> *The New Turnpike Road from New Haven to Hartford which is laid out, granted, and subscribed for, passes directly by my Door—between the house and the mill. This will be one of the most beautiful and most considerable roads in New England; being nearly in a straight line from New Haven to Hartford.*

The Cheshire Road had also been changed into a turnpike and improved. By chance or design, these roads met at Whitney's doorstep and improved both his means of communication and his public image.

Not everyone was happy about tollgates in the middle of Hamden, however. Town meetings were held, and citizens voted against them. A plea was sent to the Connecticut General Assembly, "praying [for] a removal of the Cheshire turnpike gate, established in this town so that the inhabitants can have the use of their old roads free of toll, or relief in some other manner." But the charter was solid, and nothing could be done. Turnpike companies would control the main highways for the next fifty years.

Still, although farmers despised them, these new and better roads helped business in Hamden flourish. Jonathan Mix's neighbor, Charles Brockett, manufactured his patented steel carriage springs; his was one of the first factories in the country to do so. Brockett's cooper casks were also in demand from the West Indies trade, primarily by Charles Van den Heuvel, who owned sugar estates in the West Indies but spent his summers in his mansion above the Mill River Valley. James Wyles took over Joel Munson's mill and ground corn raised in Hamden. Seymour Dickerman traded oysters to Albany with a four-horse team. A distillery opened in Mount Carmel, and a tannery appeared in Centerville. The Benham family continued to make shoes, sending their products to New Haven. Brick makers like the Johnson family helped provide material with which to build the growing towns of Connecticut. The brickyards on the east side of Hamden alone produced millions of bricks a year.

To be successful, these early entrepreneurs needed to be audacious. Whitney showed everyone the benefits of bold experimentation when he arranged the first specialized division of labor in the United States. He also translated Adam Smith's ideas of division of labor in the mechanical arena, using these ideas to make better machines. Every day he was improving and popularizing the process that would launch the Industrial Revolution. He created an entire machine-tool industry in order to make mass production possible. "In short," he said, "the tools which I contemplate are similar to an engraving on a copper plate from which may be taken a great number of impressions exactly alike." By 1801, he had developed a drilling machine, a boring machine, a screw machine and a triphammer, all of which are still used in factories today. He did not need patents because no one at the time could even figure them out. Regardless, after the cotton gin nightmare, Whitney never bothered to patent any of his inventions or methods for the rest of his life.

However, Whitney's innovations may have inspired his neighbors to do the same. Captain Jonathan Mix, hero of the Revolution, moved to Cherry Hill in southwest Hamden after his second marriage to Elizabeth Phipps and invented the elliptic brace carriage spring. He described its benefits: "The principle of the invention consists in reducing the springs of the carriage to one, and fixing that to the centre of the axle-tree and supporting the shafts on it." This ingenious device, which both strengthened and simplified the undercarriage, was immediately used in all quality stagecoaches and wagons. Mix also invented a cartridge box for ammunition and a device that helped Robert Fulton's steam frigate keep smoke away from the ship's guns. Mix did successfully patent his inventions, the benefits of which were easy for all to see.

On the other hand, it soon became clear to Whitney that no one, including the government, understood what he was doing. He could ignore the public's skepticism, but his methods of dealing with the government needed to become shrewder. When government officials claimed that his prices were too high compared to their armories, the inventor used cost-benefit analysis that included insurance and machinery to show that his way was cheaper. This type of accounting was rare at the time, and Whitney helped popularize it. But he achieved his biggest success when he traveled to Washington to demonstrate his method of interchangeability to the new president of the United States, Thomas Jefferson. Tossing a pile of random parts on a table, Whitney picked them out at random and assembled a lock. The inventor then prompted Jefferson and the others at the meeting to do the same. Jefferson assembled a gun, shocked and amazed. This had never been possible in the history of the world.

Obviously impressed, the president invested more money in the Hamden factory. More money meant more work, and Whitney threw himself into it with even more vigor. By age forty he had not had time to marry, calling himself "a solitary being, without a companion and almost without a friend." Instead, he took an interest in his nephews, Philos and Eli Whitney Blake. Through letters, he attempted to coach them in manners, dress and speech with advice like: "You will make it a solemn point…to avoid the use of profane languages." When they came of age, the two admiring boys arrived to work in Hamden with their uncle, staying in the farmhouse at Mill Rock.

By 1810, Whitney's factory in Hamden was considered "the most perfect" by the government, and the parts he produced were not only interchangeable but also judged superior. Whitney's armory was used as a model to retool

East Rock towers above the Whitney factory, with Ithiel Town's covered bridge just visible behind a tree. *Courtesy of Magnus Wahlstrom Library, University of Bridgeport.*

Springfield and Harpers Ferry. Two years later, Whitney had produced thousands of muskets for state militias and was beginning to produce weapons for the war against Britain. After a struggle with officious bureaucrats, Whitney nearly gave up, but the burning of the executive mansion and Capitol building suddenly changed their minds. Fifteen thousand guns were ordered and made, some of which were used by men from Hamden serving in the American army. Guards were posted around the factory day and night for fear of sabotage or British sneak attack.

All of this time Whitney never stopped experimenting. He figured out the importance of well-seasoned pine boxes for shipping weapons more than a century before it became common practice. He improved his machines, showing other armories how to build better triphammers. He gave away the secret to his barrel-turning machine. Then he built a power-driven mechanized cutter and created his milling machine, a "revolutionary technological advance." Instead of keeping it for himself, he simply offered the plans to other U.S. armories. It completely changed every U.S. industry.

However, the constant stress of running the factory and endless lawsuits dealing with the cotton gin debacle gave Whitney severe stomach ulcers.

When he was finally awarded a "monetary remuneration" for the cotton gin piracy, it was far less than he had spent in court to get it. For twenty years he had no private life, no leisure time. He dined and talked with the most important men of the age but had no close friends. "I have a great task before me and when I shall get through, God knows. I live constantly out at my place and tho' I have at least forty people around me every day—I am yet a solitary Old Bachelor," he said wearily. Then in 1817, at age fifty-two, he met Henrietta Edwards while on a trip to Bridgeport. Though she was twenty years younger, Whitney fell in love with her kindness and beauty. He even tried his hand at poetry to woo this granddaughter of the famous preacher Jonathan Edwards, writing:

> *And now I ask your kind permission*
> *Craving your grace with all submission*
> *If I may hope to call you mine*
> *And bless the day of St. Valentine.*

No doubt Whitney was better off sticking to invention. Nevertheless, his courting was successful, and the couple married. His nephew and namesake Eli Whitney Blake had graduated from Yale the year before and became his full-time assistant. It seemed like Whitney would finally have the family life and leisure he deserved after decades of single-minded labor.

Not that he stopped working. In 1818, he said, "I find that it is absolutely impossible for me to accomplish one half of that for which there is the most pressing necessity." The Mill Rock site had expanded to three houses, a huge barn, five stone workmen buildings and an office, with real estate in Hamden and New Haven. A small canal funneled water from the dam to the forge, and storehouses lined the canyon. Corners of the rooms collected copper tubing, blistered steel, iron, leather, asphalt, glue and squares of glass. The factory had its own lumberyard, made its own cordage and castings and forged its own steel with seven pairs of bellows and anvils. One could find a grindstone lathe, milling tools and whipsaw, drilling, screw, stamping and polishing machines—all the technology used in industry for the next two centuries. Whitney had created the first modern factory in the United States.

Nearby in New Haven, architect Ithiel Town was working on a new type of bridge. Town was one of the first generation of professional architects in the United States and had helped pioneer the Federal, Greek and Gothic Revival styles popular at the time. Avoiding the arch, which tended to "overturn the piers or abutments," Town tried a lattice truss structure. Heavy timbers

Once remarked on by President James Madison, Eli Whitney's barn still stands in Hamden today. *Courtesy of the author.*

were not needed for this bridge, and nearly anyone could construct one out of light pine planks without difficult or dangerous ironwork. It moved less than other bridges and could easily sustain a horse and carriage along a straight, unsupported span. Town explained how it worked: "The nearer those [diagonal lattice] braces are placed to each other, the more strength will the truss have." The design required no new technology, could be built by unskilled workers and might have been planned by the ancient Romans. But the first would be built in Hamden, Connecticut.

In a letter to Town in 1820, Whitney gave his advice, blessing and support to the bridge. He suggested, "This bridge may be covered to protect it from the weather, in a manner very simple, cheap, and durable…On the whole its simplicity, lightness, strength, cheapness, and durability are, in my opinion, such as to render it highly worthy of attention."

The aging inventor had given the final piece of advice that Town needed. His 1823 covered bridge over the Mill River at the intersection of the Hartford and Cheshire Turnpikes in Hamden was a huge success. This oak plank truss bridge of 114 feet would still stand today if it had been preserved.

Moreover, it became the model for thousands like it around the continent, a piece of architecture so associated with rural America that it is hard to believe someone invented it.

With his wife and four children by his side, Eli Whitney seemed to finally find success in both his business and personal lives. But in 1820 he contracted influenza, and two years later he began to have painful attacks of an unknown illness, most likely an enlarged prostate gland. He invented a flexible catheter and increased his lifespan by a couple years. However, the condition began to slow him down, and in 1822 he noted, "I am not now able to sit up more than three hours in a day." Eli Whitney Blake began supervising the shop and moved to southern Hamden, already called Whitneyville.

Eli Whitney's mind remained active and strong; he even invented a better triphammer in 1824. Nevertheless, he signed a will that left his books to his young son and gave his nephews Philos and Eli Whitney Blake control of the business. Blake would continue his uncle's tradition of experimentation and invent the mortise lock and the stone crusher. His own son, Eli Jr., would eventually take over the business he started, and it would help the North win the Civil War. Their successes eventually cleared Whitney's name as the inventor of the cotton gin, though some diehards claimed it for a variety of southern gentlemen until the twentieth century. However, we can wonder if this would have been important to the inventor in the shadow of his larger work. Using the falling water of the Mill River to drive machines of his own invention, Eli Whitney not only changed Hamden but also began the Industrial Revolution in America. And more importantly, he showed how perseverance in the face of injustice and failure could lead to greater victories and how bold experimentation could lead to progress and, in time, transform the world.

Three Sisters Against Fate

From the outset of their promising lives, the three Dickerman sisters seemed eager to seize the opportunities given them by a loving family and a growing town. Born in 1799, their father, Ezra Dickerman, had studied for the ministry briefly but instead served as the local deacon, preferring farming to a life completely in the church. He married Sarah Jones of Wallingford, and their frugal honeymoon consisted of a visit to old "Granny Bradley," who smoked a pipe. They moved into his grandfather's 1770 stone-foundation house near the Blue Hills that had a gabled roof, a central chimney and a full nine windows facing Whitney Avenue. An ancient buttonball tree sheltered the house from wind, and a tall elm shaded the barnyard. Behind the house grew huge pear, apple and hickory trees, while between the field and river a tract of first-growth trees surrounded a glacial kettle pond. As farmers, Ezra and Sarah were diligent, plowing each furrow identically and placing each seed exactly parallel.

They also concentrated on bringing up their nine children properly, with confidence and good habits, and providing an environment for learning. Aging Aunt Chloe would tell stories about living under King George and about the fierce battle in New Haven to repel British soldiers. Visitors arrived at the Dickerman homestead, like Nathaniel Taylor, first professor of the Yale Divinity School, who discussed ecclesiastical questions with Ezra; or John B. Gough, the famous temperance lecturer, who stayed with the family while on tour. Every morning, children and adults alike would gather around the crackling maple and hickory fire under a portrait of the Marquis de Lafayette to read passages from the Bible.

The three daughters of the family—Elizabeth, Abbie and Sarah—loved to read and took part in active discussions with one another, their parents and their peers. They craved knowledge and scorned the transient pleasures of fashion and entertainment. Born in 1829, Elizabeth was mild, gentle, cheerful and positive, with a keen intellect obvious to all. Two years younger, Abbie "dwelt more in her emotions" and worried about her soul. At seven years old, she wept at the fireside, telling the rest of her family that she felt like a sinner. Sarah, called "Fannie" by her family, seemed more impatient and depressed. Seven years younger than Abbie, she looked up to her sisters with both awe and fierce competiveness. All three had strong wills but did not seek attention; rather, they were reserved in their dispositions, and everyone who met them called them sweet.

Daily education included a lot of old-fashioned hard work. The three sisters were taught to make buckwheat cakes, mincemeat, hasty pudding and sausages to hang in the pantry. They helped their mother dry apples, pears and berries. Candle making, spinning and knitting had their seasons, and the Dickermans spent long hours whipping flax and sewing rag carpets. But they learned other, more amusing skills as well. Curly-haired Abbie loved riding her horse through the green woods and fields near the Blue Hills, enjoying the "gray old cliff of Carmel, the rounded slopes of the hills, the rich meadows and pastures, and the long, wood-covered mountain ranges that fringed the horizon in the distance." All three sisters learned piano and family sang songs to Elizabeth's skilled accompaniment. Along with these pursuits came a strong spiritual life. With their parents, they attended services at the Mount Carmel Congregational Church.

The settlers who founded the Congregational Church were probably the first to rename the Blue Hills "Mount Carmel." Though at that time the area was technically part of New Haven, a very distinct community grew here. Also, the farmers and hunters who lived in the shadow of this mountain were forced to travel several miles along the Quinnipiac River into North Haven to worship. So, in 1757, from the dark recesses of Bellamy's Tavern, the townsfolk wrote a successful petition to the state legislature to establish their own parish. A few months later, the Mount Carmel Ecclesiastical Society held its first meeting, but many years would pass before its questions were settled. Were they to be Presbyterian or Congregational? Would the town house the pastor? Their inability to reach agreements led to delay after delay and a series of failures to secure a spiritual leader.

Finally, in 1764, despite a no-vote majority, the church was given its lasting principles. Forty-six people stepped into the new Mount Carmel

The Mount Carmel Congregational Church, with its long carriage stables, welcomed parishioners from nearby hills and dales. *Courtesy of the Mount Carmel Congregational Church.*

Congregational Church just north of the Blue Hills. For a few years they took turns on the pulpit, until a proper minister could be found, and built their choir into something impressive. However, ten years elapsed before Reverend Sherman took over, seemingly ending the problems. Then, disappointingly, a dispute over money led to another decade of unsettled ministry. By the 1800s, the pastorate had become somewhat more settled, and when Reverend Eliphalet Coleman lasted a full thirteen years, the community sighed with relief.

This was the church that the Dickermans attended as children. Then, in 1840, a new Greek Revival building was raised across the square from the lilac bushes of Bellamy's Tavern. The bell arrived before the belfry was completed, and the practical church fathers hung it from a strong sycamore, proudly calling the Mount Carmel townsfolk to service. Inside, Corinthian pillars framed the twin doors, and the ceiling shone blue, but stained glass was voted down. In this new temple, tobacco spitting was relegated to a designated spit box. Two years later, the old New England practice of carrying hot toddies to the preacher on cold winter days was forbidden.

Members of the community attended meetings and seminars, and "a season of revival" swept through the congregation.

Though Abbie was not yet a teenager, she declared her faith. Over the next few years, she read the biographies of religious women like Harriet Winslow and Mary Lyon and began keeping a secret diary, recording her spiritual and emotional life in detail: "This evening attended singing school, and while there, felt emotions of pride. Oh, when shall I be meek and lowly in heart!" Pastor Israel Warren talked often with Abbie about "uniting with the church." Together, they convinced Elizabeth and Fannie as well, and the sisters began a regimen of prayer. They were all confirmed members of the church in the winter of 1846–47.

That year, Elizabeth left for boarding school at the Seward Institute in New York, won a scholarship and graduated with honors the next year. Abbie entered the same school the next fall but had to leave to come home to help her mother during a brief illness. However, she was able to switch places with Elizabeth and return. The older sister took charge of fifty pupils

The three Dickerman sisters—Abbie, Fannie and Elizabeth—inspired their former minister to write a book about their struggles. *Courtesy of the Hamden Historical Society.*

at a local public school, becoming instantly popular with both students and parents. In the spring of 1849, a number of Hamden notables, including the rich Ives family, requested that the admired and well-educated sisters open their own school.

This was not the first time a private school had been considered by the town. In Bellamy's Tavern, where all important business seemed to be conducted, the founding of an Episcopal Academy in Connecticut had been discussed in 1794. However, nearby Cheshire had been chosen rather than Hamden. Then, the Reverend Charles William Everest founded a seminary for boys in 1843. From a population of nine students and a black Newfoundland dog, the Rectory School grew to an enrollment of sixty-five, which was set as the "maximum desired." The students wore West Point gray and could be seen marching up and down the avenue; this was the first boys' school in the nation to implement military drills.

No doubt this success inspired Mount Carmel's new seminary for girls. Elizabeth opened her classes in a private home nearby, but so many applied that her wealthy patrons built a new school on the hill above the Cheshire Turnpike, a half mile from the church. The two-story building, with its clapboard siding, cupola and bell, only took a few months to build. Elizabeth occupied it in February 1850, and forty pupils began attending immediately. The sisters' lively group of friends in Mount Carmel helped out, and when Abbie returned from the Seward Institute, she joined them. The sisters had focused their spiritual beliefs through hard work and now struggled to improve the entire community.

Many girls came from New Haven and Meriden to attend. However, a few boys were allowed, such as the Dickermans' younger brothers Ezra, George and Watson. Youngest sister Fannie also attended and then assisted teaching the youngest pupils. Abbie briefly taught in New Britain. The students were not used to work and misbehaved terribly, running away from school and talking back to her. She was forced to apply "the rod" and had many conversations with God about this controversial practice. When her contract ended, she returned to the seminary in Hamden.

At this time, Hamden experienced breakouts of epidemic dysentery, and pastor Israel Warren's only daughter died. Abbie knew the child well and felt a huge blow. "Last Monday we followed the remains of dear little Jennie to the grave, and saw her beautiful form consigned to the narrow tomb," she wrote. Abbie also caught dysentery and spent several weeks in bed and by the fire. Upon her recovery, she felt well enough to ride as far as Centerville, declaring that evening, "I do thirst for knowledge; and when I think of the fields of science which lie before me, I long to explore them, and make acquisitions there which will last for ever." However, exploration would have to be left for others. The troubles with her liver soon developed into the dreaded plague of the nineteenth century: consumption.

By June 1851, Abbie seemed to know that her time was short: "I often think that my days here are nearly spent." But she never lost her gratitude for the gifts she had received. "As I sit by my window," she wrote, "looking out upon this beautiful world, now clothed in its richest verdure, every thing seems to repeat the same utterances of love and joy." She remained sick and in bed until the next year, hair chopped short and cheeks sunken. In addition to consumption, the doctor diagnosed a disease of the spine and lungs. By the following summer, she was suffering terrible pain on a daily basis and could no longer write letters or the secret journal that her family soon discovered.

Inspired by Abbie's example, Elizabeth began to keep her own journal. The first entry on August 1, 1852, expresses a wish "to do what I can to fill the vacant place which will soon be made by her death in our family circle." In another notation, she bravely confessed, "Have been with father to select a burial place for her." Elizabeth sat with her sister after school each day. Once, Abbie wiped tears from her face, saying, "It is hard to part," and hugged her sister. But she also breathed, "I am happy, happy now." A few days later, she motioned to be moved to the window to see the beautiful landscape of Hamden, dying hours afterward at the age of twenty-one from a pulmonary hemorrhage. Her sisters grieved, but they did not grieve alone. The rest of the Mount Carmel congregation helped the family work through their pain, something seen as a community responsibility.

A multitude of churches now took on these responsibilities in Hamden and provided a rich spiritual life for the growing town. After moving to Hamden following the Revolution, Captain Jonathan Mix held church services at his home for those who could not make the long trek up to Mount Carmel or down into New Haven. He also helped to establish the East Plains Congregational Church in 1795. In 1834, the wonderful Greek Revival–style Whitneyville Church had been built on the banks of the Mill River to replace it, on land donated by Eli Whitney's widow and son. Four years later, Reverend Austin Putnam began his ministry there, one that would continue for almost fifty years. And of course it was not only Congregationalists who made Hamden their home. The Mount Carmel Episcopalians had organized in 1790, and by 1812 their church was built. However, few attended these services, and by 1819 they had moved their assembly to Centerville, into the beautiful Grace

Episcopal Church with its clapboard walls and Ionic colonnade. The man who named the town, Amasa Bradley, served as lay reader for twenty-five years. Separatists and Methodists moved into Hamden, as well, and by 1810 they were well established. By 1817, a Baptist Society had been founded. Though these sects had differing doctrines, all inspired faith and service and connected the many villages of Hamden in new ways.

Elizabeth's own connections with others and desire to serve became even more pronounced after Abbie died. She played the new piano that her father brought home but found less pleasure than anticipated. She went back to teach that autumn: "Never before have I so felt the responsibility resting on me as a teacher." Hard work and engagement with the world would be the cure, for there was no asceticism in Elizabeth's beliefs. Though mindful of her duties, she always smiled and joked with her family and friends. She paid special attention to her remaining sister, Fannie.

The youngest Dickerman sister loved books and read aloud to her mother and grandmother whenever given the chance. While her mother did housework, Fannie would follow her mother around to ask questions about her reading. Her quest for knowledge was matched by a desire for perfectionism, and her gift for writing exceeded her sisters. As a young girl attending the Mount Carmel Female Seminary, she wrote a composition so strong that it was disqualified from the prize as the work of an adult. Her flaw was her irritability. Once, after yelling at her younger brother, Ezra Day, she said, "Oh, when shall I learn to govern this wicked temper?" She wrote him a letter asking forgiveness, signed "from your wicked, but sorry sister, Fannie."

In 1853, the former Mount Carmel pastor, Israel Warren, invited Elizabeth to be the principal of another female seminary in Plymouth, Connecticut. While Elizabeth was away, Fannie often visited Abbie's grave, placing on it spring wildflowers from the slopes of the Blue Hills. She taught at the Mount Carmel Female Seminary. When she visited Elizabeth in July, her older sister noticed a persistent cough. It lingered, and no remedies seemed to take effect. Soon, it was clear that the disease that had taken her sister was affecting her. In August, Elizabeth came home from summer session and immediately rushed to the bedroom. Fannie was sitting by the window, wrapped in a white, loose dress, looking pale and thin. Elizabeth saw in her face the same look that Abbie had, and after a quick kiss hello, she ran out of the room and burst into tears. During her five weeks of vacation she tended Fannie, preparing wonderful meals, picking flowers and riding in the family carriage with her. Fannie seemed to improve, and her overly passionate temperament changed for the better.

Returning to school in September, Elizabeth found that her duties had increased to principal and matron, cooking codfish and soda biscuits, cleaning and washing. With only four pupils attending, she wished to be home. "Here am I away from all that are near and dear to me—for what?" But more students soon showed up, and with thirty-two scholars things looked better. She hoped Fannie would join her as a teacher in the spring, writing, "I feel that I am engaged in a noble work." Elizabeth returned home for Christmas and found that Fannie had relapsed. Her journal reads, "Fannie was poorly fitted to buffet the trials of life...when I realize that I shall soon be left without a sister, it seems so hard—but it is better to have sisters in heaven than sisters on earth."

Fannie's limbs swelled, and she developed bedsores from lying too long in bed. On Sunday, January 8, 1854, Fannie had two hemorrhages, and on Tuesday evening her lungs began to bleed. She coughed for an hour straight but afterward was able to take a snack. "How nice these peaches are," she said, and a little while later she declared, "My love to all, good-by." Her younger brothers Ezra Day and George sat weeping by the bed. "Boys," she said weakly, "learn your lessons well, and try to understand them." Their father sang a hymn as she died. "I can not weep for her today. The fountain of my tears is dried up," Elizabeth wrote a few days later on Friday the thirteenth.

Elizabeth could not return immediately to the Plymouth seminary after this second loss. She rested at home but could not remain idle and rode her horse up and down Whitney Avenue. No doubt she found instructive interest at the beautiful Grace Episcopal Church and Rectory School in Centerville, by this time "one of the leading military boarding schools in new England." They had expanded to a dozen buildings, including a boathouse on the Mill River, and had become famous in the region.

Fame would soon become a curse for the school. During the Civil War, some pupils from the South rebelled against the headmaster's authority, and one was expelled. A tough officer from the Thirteenth New York Cavalry came in as an instructor and stopped the insurgence cold. However, in 1863, a fire ruined the playhouse and gashouse. Five years later, the barn burned, and since someone had tampered with the lock, three horses and all of the equipment inside was lost. Then a fire broke out in the attic of the main house. At first these incidents were thought to be accidental, but a few days later, on October 3, the schoolhouse burst into flame, nearly suffocating the sleeping students. The playhouse flared up four days later. The following day, the schoolhouse was drenched in kerosene and set on fire for the second time.

The Rectory School became the first of many opportunities for private education in Hamden. *Courtesy of Magnus Wahlstrom Library, University of Bridgeport.*

At last a homesick pupil was caught, arrested and expelled. A new barn was designed and built by famous architect Henry Austin. But both the campus and reputation of the Rectory School suffered. The rash of destructive pyromania made national headlines. Then a malaria epidemic in nearby New Haven caused publicity problems, and in January 1873 the school closed. "It's growing dark now! The school is dismissed," an aging Dr. Everest wrote, completing the record book thirty years after he had begun his ambitious project.

However, Elizabeth was not to see any of that future. She eventually rode back to Plymouth and continued the hard work of teaching that had been her life. Weakened by her struggles and grief, she became ill herself. "I am distressed that I am causing so much trouble about the school…Another can fill my place here, but none can be a daughter to my parents." On April 12, after exams, she left for home in time for her twenty-sixth birthday, "and so little accomplished," she wrote. "It seems but a few days since dear Abbie was instructing a class just in front of mine, and Fannie was one of my pupils." She set her mind to staying well. Visiting a friend in Hartford, she "had a most delightful sail up the beautiful Connecticut. I was almost too happy. I was glad to be alone, for I longed to drink in every beauty as we passed." She rode a horse around the state capital, able to enjoy life again. That summer of 1855, her father built another barn, and Elizabeth helped, drawing plans and working to make the space livable and beautiful. She seemed to be able to do anything she put her mind to. She received an invitation to teach in Harrisburg, Pennsylvania, and her love of teaching was "kindled anew."

The Mount Carmel Female Seminary stands high on a hill above Whitney Avenue, a testament to faith and learning. *Courtesy of the Hamden Historical Society.*

Then, during a visit with friends, Elizabeth had an attack of abdominal pain. She went into the care of a skilled nurse in New Haven, but her suffering grew worse. By May 1856, she had been sent home pale and weak, with all hope lost. She sat by the open window where Abbie had sat four years earlier to view the beautiful valley of the Mill River. But her vigil did not last long. A violent attack of acute pain lasted for over an hour, and the next morning she died at age twenty-seven, the last daughter of two parents who had seen their share of grief. An outpouring of sympathy and support from family, church and friends helped them through the tragedy—because that is what communities do best, absorb the pain of our wounds and strengthen our resolve in the face of adversity. They teach us to balance faith and work, pleasure and education. And they nurture our spirits so that in both living and passing we may find a little of the grace attained by those three lost sisters of Mount Carmel.

CHAPTER 4

The Shape of Things to Come

Hamden was forged by war and industry, and some of America's finest citizens settled here. But it was not a one-way street. Many children and grandchildren of the original settlers had moved west to settle Litchfield, the Berkshires, Vermont, Pennsylvania, the Hudson Valley, Ohio and far-off Minnesota. One of those pioneers was Jairus Dickerman, grandson of the Jonathan Dickerman who built his house at the base of the Sleeping Giant. Jairus married Phoebe Boynton, part of an influential political family, while his son Sumner became a painter and undertook an 1840s expedition across the United States. Sumner's life-sized portraits of Native American life, colored by hand in tents and wigwams, were placed in the Smithsonian Institute only to be lost in a terrible fire. However, this forgotten painter would not be the only famous seed of Hamden to grow in other lands. Two other transplants would help shape the art of the entire nineteenth century: Henry Austin and Chauncey Ives.

Born the son of Daniel and Adah Austin in 1804, Henry began carpentry work at age fifteen, learning the mechanics of building amongst the heavy-framed, hewn-oak houses of colonial Hamden. When Ithiel Town's truss bridge first spanned the Mill River in the 1820s, it no doubt spurred this carpenter to thoughts of the possibilities of architecture. A short, stocky man, Austin worked tirelessly, learning his trade at a time when no school of architecture existed in America. He read hundreds of books and met Ithiel Town and studied his style. As the leading architect in the nation, Town quickly had a "very high opinion" of Austin's "tastes and talents."

Henry began practice in the 1830s and opened an office in New Haven in 1837. In April 1838, he drew up plans to complete the tower of Christ Church Cathedral in Hartford. Traveling back and forth between these two Connecticut cities, Austin drummed up business as a master of many styles: Gothic, Indian, Rococo, Grecian and Italianate. He also began to develop an eclectic mingling of forms and designs all his own. There were personal setbacks, but by 1841 he had firmly taken root in New Haven, and his career as an independent architect was secure. Though a high-strung, touchy man, Ithiel Town was generous and allowed the much younger Austin to work with him on Hartford's Wadsworth Athenaeum, America's oldest public art museum. It may have been a sign that Austin had received the famous draftsman's symbolic pen. When Town died a few years later, Austin did in fact inherit part of his architecture library, at the time the largest in the entire world.

Austin's first large commission on his own was probably for the Yale Library in 1842. Using brown sandstone, Austin built it in the Gothic Revival style with a church-like spire, setting the mode for much of Yale's future appearance. He also began designing houses all over New England in what critics of the day called "modernized Gothic" and "suitable for a rural city, a village, or for the country." But Austin did not stick to one style or even one form. In 1846, he designed a monument to Connecticut's war hero, Nathan Hale. Set in Hale's hometown of Coventry, the obelisk weighed 125 tons and commemorated his famous line: "I only regret that I have but one life to lose for my country."

Another Hamden native would also memorialize the American Revolution in stone. Chauncey Bradley Ives was one of seven children born to Jared and Sylvia Ives in a large, two-story farmhouse that later stood at the corner of Elm Street and Linden Avenue. His lungs were tubercular and weak, and he could not help his farming family as much as he would have liked. Though the Yankees of New England often looked down on the arts, Ives left his Hamden home at sixteen to apprentice himself to Rodolphus Northrop, a wood carver. Upon finishing this apprenticeship, he moved on to Hezekiah Augur, the leading sculptor in Connecticut, to learn to carve marble.

Ives set off for Boston at age twenty-seven, the same year Austin opened his own studio. There he locked himself in a rented room and carved busts from marble unassisted by clay or model. One of these busts was displayed in a jeweler's window and brought Ives his first business. He exhibited his neoclassical-style sculptures in Boston and was doing well, but his consumptive tendencies continued to plague him. While in Meriden, at age thirty-one, a doctor took him aside and prescribed a warmer climate. He refused but, three years later, conceded the doctor's point and left the winters of New England for Florence, Italy, where he became one of the most successful American expatriate sculptors of the nineteenth century.

While Ives and Austin were shaping stone, the shape of their hometown would change as well. Three main paths approached Hamden from New Haven. In the plains area of the southwest, Dixwell Avenue formed the main northern artery, eventually turning east to cross the second artery— the Cheshire Turnpike, sometimes called Whitney Avenue—which passed north through Whitneyville, Centerville and Mount Carmel on its way to Cheshire, Farmington and beyond. The Hartford Turnpike left Whitney Avenue near the arms factory and shot straight northeast, forming part of the eastern border of town, except in the southeast, where the third artery, State Street, wound around salt marshes, passing into North Haven and eventually meeting the Hartford road. To the west of Dixwell and Whitney Avenues, Pine Rock, Dunbar Hill, High Rock and West Woods all fell within Hamden's boundaries, hemmed on that side by the long ridges West Rock, Mad Mare's Hill and Mount Sanford.

By the time the two artists were children, many of the original forests in this territory had been cut down, replaced by farmland, peach orchards and acres of mulberry trees for silk production. The Mill River had been dammed in both the south and north, and mills utilized its current. Falling streams were dammed near Hamden Plains and in West Woods, though as the nineteenth century progressed, the mills grew fewer, and many small dams disappeared. The land had also been mined for copper, with shafts dug into Ridge Hill north of the Sleeping Giant and on the mountain itself.

The ambitious project of the Farmington Canal was doomed by the arrival of the railroad. *Courtesy of the Hamden Historical Society.*

However, not enough ore was found to pay for the expense of digging, and the deep shafts were left abandoned.

These projects had transformed the landscape since colonial times. But in the 1820s, "canal fever" struck the eastern United States, and Hamden would change again. Entrepreneurs planned a canal from New Haven to Farmington and farther on to Northampton, Massachusetts. Eli Whitney Blake actually made a preliminary survey, and investors salivated at the prospect of taking business through New Haven and away from the Connecticut River. Work started on the Farmington Canal in 1825, and two years later workers dug through Cheshire and Hamden. The sandy earth of southern Hamden gave the builders trouble, but using clay solved the problem. This channel angled from Pine Swamp through Hamden Plains to Centerville, changing direction and spearing directly north, parallel to Whitney Avenue. By June 1828, the channel reached from end to end in Hamden, and the lock keeper's houses were opened.

Two years later, this inland waterway was fully operational, bringing business to places like the Red Tavern in Hamden Plains and Bellamy's Tavern in Mount Carmel. Amasa Bradley's house also converted to a tavern serving aquatic travelers, with a boat basin nearby that allowed them to tie up and visit his basement taproom. In 1838, the New Haven Packet Boat Company took passengers up the canal to Northampton, Massachusetts, in twenty-six hours for the steep price of $3.75, including meals. On September 14, 1839, African mutineers from the slave ship *Amistad* passed through Hamden on the canal. The citizens all lined the path to see these brave and exotic African men before they went to trial.

Within a decade, the canal had become a fixed part of the Hamden landscape. People skated on the canal during winter and bathed in it during summer. Places like Kimberly's Store at the Steps now took in a booming business from the brightly painted packet boats, as well as from road travelers. Not everyone was happy, though. Homes had been removed to make way for the channel, and it cut through dozens of farms and yards. Even though business along the canal boomed, the costs to maintain it during seasons of flood and drought turned out to be greater. The stockholders who invested in developers like the Hampshire and Hampden Company never prospered, and the canal fever seemed over before it had begun.

Though Henry Austin now lived on George Street in New Haven, he did not ignore the changes in his hometown. He designed several houses and a steeple for Grace Church. When the church's Rectory Barn was burned, he designed a new one. One of the houses he built here was Stick

Henry Austin's plans for Dwight Hall would shape the architecture of Yale University for the next century. *Courtesy of Magnus Wahlstrom Library, University of Bridgeport.*

Style, a Victorian version of a Gothic cottage. Its elaborate porch, Swiss chalet elements and patterned end panels made it unique in the Highwood neighborhood. It is remarkable that Austin found any time at all for Hamden, since he was certainly becoming the most in-demand architect in the Northeast.

Working outside the mainstream of American architecture, Austin interpreted styles in his own exotic way, building on the past but also looking to the future. He designed churches without dogma: Episcopal cathedrals in Hartford, Seymour and Waterbury; Congregational meetinghouses in Northford, Danbury, Kent, Portland and Plainville; and a Presbyterian church in Trenton, New Jersey. He designed the Bowdoin College chapel and the Rich Library at Wesleyan. Nothing seemed beyond his reach: banks, institutes, schools and houses in Connecticut, Maine, New Jersey and Massachusetts. He planned whole developments, like Trenton Row in New Jersey and Ravenswood on Long Island. He did not ignore New Haven, and it seemed there was a grand Austin house on every street. In 1859, he remodeled Ithiel Town's Hillhouse Avenue mansion, turning it into an Italianate villa. He also built the Davies House in 1868, a "grand-towered Italian villa" that had a view of all of New Haven. His most daring design was for city hall—a green, Victorian-Gothic monster with a clock tower and iron staircase illuminated by a skylight.

As an old man, celebrated architect Henry Austin insisted on wearing his hairpiece at all times. *Courtesy of the Hamden Historical Society.*

Austin no longer needed to advertise for clients and could relax a little in his fame. He could often be seen around town in his black, broadcloth frock coat and brown wig. He sat on the New Haven City Council in 1854, became an expert marksman and spent time at the Masonic lodge. By now he had moved on to his second wife and had fathered many children. However, it was as "Father of Architects" that he found lasting fame, having trained dozens in his studio in New Haven over the decades, including his own son Fred. Though New Haven was physically only a few miles away from his hometown, it was a different world for this poor carpenter from Hamden, now the toast of Connecticut.

Chauncey Ives had traveled much farther, though he came back to the United States several times for exhibitions and commissions. From Florence, in 1851 he moved to Rome and found work in the courtyard of an artist's colony house. In 1854, he carved *Pandora*, shown just at the moment she is opening the jar that will let loose sin on the world. This sculpture was a huge attraction in the New York City exhibition of 1855. Soon afterward, he exhibited a real masterpiece, *Undine Receiving Her Soul*, with a technically amazing thin "wet" veil hanging over the up-stretched figure. His mastery of detailed surface patterns stunned both the public and Ives's contemporaries.

Back in Rome, Ives married Maria Davis from Brooklyn and sired seven children. Now famous amongst the expatriate Americans in Italy, they lived a good life in the warm Mediterranean climate. Soon Ives carved a bust of Austin's predecessor, Ithiel Town, which many considered his finest work.

His *Willing Captive* showed the real historical incident of a New England girl refusing to return to her begging mother, preferring her Indian husband. His reputation was built, however, on his skill in representing childhood, as in *Flower Girl* and *Rebecca at the Well*, both now housed at the Metropolitan Museum of Art. The tender portraits of these vulnerable girls often moved nineteenth-century viewers to tears. We can only wonder how Ives's own youth in Hamden influenced his ability to capture the inner lives of children so beautifully.

By the 1870s, the neoclassical sculptures were "on the wane," but Ives continued to work. His statues were said to represent "the taste of his generation," with "Hellenistic grace" and "serenity." In his old age, he was given a commission by the government of the United States and carved Jonathan Trumbull and Roger Sherman, two of Connecticut's Patriots, for Statuary Hall in Washington, D.C. Like Austin before him, he was shaping the Nutmeg State's legacy, even though he would never return.

Hamden itself may have been unrecognizable to Ives by then anyway. In 1850, blight devastated the peach orchards, and except for a few holdouts like Waite Chatterton's, the mills had all closed. A new carpet of trees had grown over large portions of the landscape, and many colonial farms had

Chauncey Ives's statue *Pandora* shows the moment her curiosity gets the better of her and she releases evil on the world. *Courtesy of Marian O'Keefe, Barnum Museum, Bridgeport, Connecticut.*

disappeared into the soil. In Mount Carmel, willow trees had grown tall around the dammed lake, while chestnuts and hickories had overtaken the slopes of the Sleeping Giant. On Spruce Bank above the Mill River, an ample crown of hemlocks cast huge shadows, seeming to grow backward into wilderness even as other parts of the town moved forward into industry.

The landscape of southern Hamden had changed entirely when Eli Whitney Jr. built a new dam by his factory, thirty-eight feet high, spreading a huge lake two miles north that contained more than 500 million gallons of water. Three old mills were submerged, and roads and bridges had to be moved. Engineers claimed that Ithiel Town's old bridge was too heavy to be moved, but Whitney took after his father and did it anyway, crafting chestnut ribs, sills and rollers to send it up the road to Davis Street. The procedure only cost $250. And although the entire damming operation ended as a loss, the factory was producing so many firearms that it absorbed the losses easily. Whitney Jr. eventually organized the New Haven Water Company to serve the city's need for water and raised the dam at Mill Rock even higher, submerging a huge area between Whitneyville and Centerville.

However, the largest change to the town was the early death of the Farmington Canal. When the waterway was in its last throes, a desperate appeal to save it was made to the U.S. Congress, but it fell on deaf ears. The canal had never been profitable, and railroads were the future. The Hartford and New Haven line had been completed along State Street as far back as 1838, but another railway was built in 1848 on the bones of the old canal. After all, the towpath was already graded, and though this line paralleled the first, it reached into Cheshire, New Britain and Farmington. By the 1850s,

To put the canal and railroad through Mount Carmel, engineers had to cut through "the Steps." *Courtesy of the Hamden Historical Society.*

iron engines were chugging up and down Whitney Avenue, and the canal was a distant memory.

A traveler from Hamden could now hop the train at Mount Carmel station and ride into New Haven. Arriving at Union Station on the west side of the platform, she would walk up the stairs from the tracks, amazed by the suspended platform and hanging walkways. Over three hundred feet in length, the station included luxurious parlors where she could find comfort before walking outside to marvel at its two spires reaching over one hundred feet in the air. More an Italian villa than a train depot, Union Station was one of Henry Austin's most majestic works, and no one who stopped there could ignore it.

Though Austin had found success, as he aged he became tired of the daily business of the firm. His son Fred, who trained for eighteen years with him, eventually took over, renaming the firm Henry Austin and Son. For ten more years, Henry saw new generations of architects make their own marks, designing a new world as strange to him as his would have been to the pioneers who had first settled Hamden. In 1845, this Father of Architects had designed the enormous Egyptian gateway to the Grove Street Cemetery, and nearly forty years later he found life's only permanence within its walls. Chauncey Ives's sculptures had already passed out of style by the time he was laid to rest far away in Rome, while one thousand other offshoots of the Hamden tree lay buried and unknown in every corner of this new world. After all, settlers become unsettled, new generations find new frontiers and even art cannot show us the shape of things to come.

CHAPTER 5

The Courage to Serve

Ezra Day Dickerman grew up in Mount Carmel, where his older sisters Elizabeth, Abbie and Fannie taught him while they could in the seminary school. The farm taught him both the value of work and the beauty of nature. Their neighbor, Jared Atwater, was acknowledged as a master carpenter, and Ezra learned the trade from him, building a small shop of his own at the farm to craft sleds and carriages. Soon, the Dickerman house and barn brimmed with his useful creations. When he could ride a horse, Ezra could be seen galloping up and down the long stretch of the old Cheshire Turnpike, now renamed Whitney Avenue. No doubt due to his sisters' influence, he began teaching at the grammar school in Hamden, and he often steered his horse into the hills of West Woods or to the far side of the Sleeping Giant to teach youngsters the word of God. His path would no doubt be the same as his dearly loved sisters, leading him to serve in the halls of secular and spiritual education.

Meanwhile, Ezra's older brothers, Edward and "Street" Dickerman, had migrated to Illinois. Once, Street sent a letter home with a small picture of Abe Lincoln, whom he said would be a candidate for the presidency. Little did adolescent Ezra know that this man would be the most important American president since George Washington and that his own life would be utterly transformed by the events of the next few years. This became apparent when Southern rebels attacked Fort Sumter in 1861, shortly after Abe was voted president. Young men from all over the North signed up immediately. What could Ezra do?

His father, for whom he had been named, had died the previous year. His sisters were gone. No doubt shattered by the death of her husband

This house where "the three sisters" and Ezra Day Dickerman grew up still stands today. In front, Ezra Day's mother and brother pose with a wagon that he constructed. *Courtesy of Magnus Wahlstrom Library, University of Bridgeport.*

and three daughters, Ezra's mother did not want her son to leave. She may have imagined him finishing the important work the family had started in Hamden. But perhaps the young man knew, even then, that his destiny was to serve his fellow man in a different way. "I must go," he told her firmly. Finally, after the disastrous Battle of Bull Run, when Abraham Lincoln called for "300,000 more," his reluctant mother consented.

Twenty-one-year-old Ezra enlisted on September 7, 1861, in Company A of the soon-to-be-famous Connecticut Tenth. Ezra's captain, Benjamin Pardee, was also from Hamden. Captain Pardee described the Sunday meeting in New Haven just before departure:

> *The men are grouped about in easy postures and their mobile features express clearly the emotions of the hour. Close on one side rushes by the heavily-laden train, jarring the earth in its passage; on the other comes from a camp the steady, monotonous drum-beat. The bayonets of our sentries glitter coldly in the moonlight; and white and frosty, as if snow-clad, shine the long lines of the encampment.*

The men sang songs and spoke warmly of their families, but it would be four long years before many would see their homes again.

They headed south to retake the sandbar forts off North Carolina. Captain Pardee described the long misery aboard transports. "The skies black unpromising; the surf beating sullenly the solemn requiem of the lost; sickness on all the vessels; epidemics rapidly extending; deaths frequent; no comforts for the sick; scanty food for the well; water, tainted with kerosene, served out in limited quantities." It was a brutal introduction to the suffering of war for Ezra and the men of Hamden. Luckily, the amphibious operation was successful, and the Tenth and the rest of the Union army landed on the beaches. They slogged forward through the swamps, pushing back Confederate skirmishers. Pardee wrote: "When we debouched from the road into the cleared way, it brought us right in front of the rebel guns, and in perfect range." Despite having never been under fire before, the boys from Connecticut held the line. In the midst of the action, a bullet smacked Ezra in the chin, nearly breaking his jaw. But the young soldier shrugged it off, returning immediately to his company after being bandaged. This "bravery" attracted attention from his officers, who also noted his "promptness, soldierly appearance and conduct, and studious habits." Shortly after Roanoke Island was taken, Ezra was promoted to corporal and then to second lieutenant. He had passed the first test of his courage.

Of course, Ezra was not the only man from Hamden to fight in the Civil War. They served in almost every regiment of the Union. Benjamin Woodin worked at Hamden's Augur Shop and the Candee Factory as one of the first men in the world to craft rubber shoes. But he gave up his job and enlisted in the Twenty-fourth with a number of Hamden men. Mrs. Clarence E. Shepard's uncle served in the Union army and, like so many others, had to struggle with the thought of fighting relatives from the South. She remembered him telling her mother, "If I see 'em, I won't kill 'em, but I may wing them, or at least I won't let 'em do anything to our people." And Samuel Craft, a prominent brick maker on State Street, gave up his business to become a captain in the navy, helping to take Fort Fisher in North Carolina.

Back in Hamden, the townspeople did all they could to support the war. Soldiers' aid societies sent the men food packages and sewed uniforms. At a meeting of the electors in 1862, the town decided to pay a reward of $200 for each man who enlisted during the war. The popular first selectman, Charles Brockett, who had manufactured wagon springs before the war, guided Hamden through this difficult time. He prevented useless litigation and helped settle the townspeople when drafts were called. Morale amongst the townspeople was kept up by a series of livestock fairs, with attractions such as J.J. Webb's full-ton bull and a pumpkin that weighed 280 pounds.

Though fun was occasionally to be had, no one could forget the war. Eli Whitney's son had already used the old factory to make firearms for Samuel Colt.

By the time the Civil War began, Hamden was producing thirty thousand guns a year for the United States government. Now, a prominent shirt manufacturer named Oliver Winchester was using Whitney's armory to develop the famed Henry rifle, which used fixed ammunition instead of a ball and paper cartridge. Breech-loaded, it used a brass case cartridge with a conical fixed head. More accurate and more easily loaded than the Springfield, and more far ranging than the Sharps, it quickly became a favorite amongst infantrymen who could afford to buy their own guns. One of the largest gun manufacturers in the North, the armory employed hundreds of men, many of whom moved their families to the thriving Whitneyville.

Two women from Hamden—Sylvia Doolittle and her adopted daughter, Sarah Chadwick—left Mount Carmel to volunteer as nurses, following Dorothea Dix's and Clara Barton's examples. This male-dominated profession scoffed at the newcomers, believing that at best they would get in the way and at worst would "lose moral virtue." Sylvia and Sarah also struggled against official condemnations of their profession but remained true to their pioneering service until the end of the war.

Women were not the only Americans now able to test their courage. William Singleton did not reside in Hamden until after the war but began his life as a slave in North Carolina. Assigned as a servant to a Confederate officer, he ran away and met the Connecticut Tenth with seven other escapees. Wanting to do his part, he organized a regiment of one thousand African Americans from North Carolina. He traveled to Washington, D.C., to meet Abraham Lincoln and ask for an official Federal sanction to fight. Lincoln told him, "Pluck have you, but it is out of my power to grant your request… hold onto your 'club' until you may." When Lincoln signed the Emancipation Proclamation, Congress passed a bill that organized Singleton's regiment as the Thirty-fifth U.S. Infantry. The situation of free men of color in the North abruptly changed as well. The Connecticut Twenty-ninth filled with African American volunteers, while more joined the Thirtieth. Black men like James Jackson from Hamden joined them, twenty-one in all, to fight for what was now their people's chance at freedom and equality. Jackson and his comrades sailed for the South, destined for the Siege of Petersburg, where they would spend months engaged in that brutal struggle.

Meanwhile, other new regiments were forming in the state, and Ezra's brother Edward Dickerman came all the way from Illinois to help raise a company from Hamden. Ezra was transferred to this unit in the Connecticut Twentieth and, by popular vote, was promoted again to become captain. Eli Whitney Jr. presented him with one hundred revolvers, saying, "May you ever bear in mind the righteousness and justice of your cause, and that you are fighting for the nobility of labor and for civil liberty." Ezra thanked his benefactor, replying:

> *In seeking a name for this company, we have found none under which we can more enthusiastically contend for the holy cause in which we are enlisted, than that which you bear—a name not only associated with the interests of, and honored by the town of Hamden and the county of New Haven, but the state and the whole nation.*

Now called the Whitney Rifles, this group of old friends and neighbors trained at Oyster Point and, on September 11, 1862, left New Haven with their regiment amidst cheering and the music of military bands. It would be three long years before these brave Hamden men returned.

By the spring of 1863, Ezra and his fellow soldiers were in Virginia. One night they marched through the darkness across a river and through a swamp toward Chancellorsville. Once there, they dug trenches with bayonets and dinner plates. Advancing, Captain Dickerman led his untried men into

Major Ezra Day Dickerman was lauded for his bravery numerous times, taking several wounds in defense of the Union. *Courtesy of the Bridgeport Public Library Historical Collections.*

fire for the first time. The next day, the enemy soldiers attacked in force, yelling at the top of their lungs: "Come in out of the cold, Yanks!" A fierce battle followed, ending in a military disaster for the boys from Connecticut. Though Confederate general Stonewall Jackson lay dead, the Connecticut Twenty-seventh was almost entirely captured, and Ezra's regiment lost a third of its number. Many were killed, and more suffered wounds, including Ezra, who was shot in the hip.

Ezra was sent back to Bridgeport, where the famous surgeon Robert Hubbard treated him. He also met his future wife, Mary Louise Lacey, who no doubt fell hard for this heroic war veteran. Nevertheless, he itched to return to his company, a feeling that intensified when rumors began to fly about the coming battle in Pennsylvania. Though his doctors protested, Ezra quickly jumped the train to Washington, trying desperately to find where his regiment was stationed. Without clear directions, he climbed onto a pork barrel on a supply train bound for the town of Westminster, Maryland, twenty-five miles from Gettysburg. Despite his wounded hip, he walked the entire distance from the train depot, reporting for duty to his shocked commanders. When asked why he had gone to such lengths, he said, "I promised the boys to stand by them, and knew they would want me with them." Five minutes later, hostilities erupted on the most terrible day of battle in American history.

His company had taken the extreme right flank in a precarious position near Rock Creek. Throughout July 1 and 2, the men "lay in line of battle in a cornfield, ready at a moment's notice." At 5:00 a.m. on the third, the regiment attacked, took possession of a stone wall and passed it. The battle raged back and forth for hours, until finally the Rebels opposing them fled. Ezra and the Whitney Rifles had "restored the line" by 11:00 a.m. and then reinforced the hard-pressed Fourteenth, Seventeenth and Twenty-seventh in the afternoon, moving through heavy fire again and again. Finally, as the day limped to a close in the yellow haze of gunpowder smoke, the Confederate lines broke and fled. "Victory, victory!" cried out the Yankee troops, exhausted and relieved. Though this fateful battle had saved the Union, thousands upon thousands had died, including Joel C. Dickerman, Ezra's cousin, who lay motionless on the banks of Rock Creek.

After Gettysburg, Dickerman's regiment marched to Tennessee to guard the railroads. Following General Ulysses S. Grant over the mountains to Georgia, the Connecticut men defended the supplies from frequent guerrilla attacks. Grant defeated the forces at Lookout Mountain while the members of the Whitney Rifles patrolled the roads. When Sherman took over for Grant in the spring of 1864, the Twentieth gathered in Lookout Valley for a push toward Atlanta. On May 8, Sherman tried but failed to get through the mountain passes north of the city. So at midnight the Union troops marched four miles in the dark. Then, skirmishers directly under Captain Dickerman advanced in a double line, quickly hustling through the dark forest, almost capturing the Confederate's entire picket line. By 8:00 a.m. the Whitney Rifles had chased the Rebels off the trail up to the mountain peak. They encircled the enemy and held the pass until May 11, when they were relieved.

A few days later, they fought in the Battle of Resaca under heavy grapeshot and canister fire. Then the Nineteenth Michigan and Twentieth Connecticut, with no other help, fixed their bayonets and, in a bitter battle, captured the town of Cassville. Ezra was again commended for "promptness and good conduct." Finally, on June 17, the Whitney Rifles crossed the Chattahoochee River and Peach Tree Creek near Atlanta. Under heavy fire they took a ravine, repelling a desperate attack. They pushed the Rebels steadily back across a hill, firing 150 rounds of ammunition each.

Here Ezra fell, hit in the temple by a rifle ball. When he was dragged back behind the lines, the battlefield surgeons pronounced this third war wound hopeless and left him to die. But while Sherman and the rest of the regiment marched into Atlanta, one of Dickerman's friends from Hamden frantically arranged for his transport back to Nashville. Thirteen days passed as Ezra was carried through the mountains, slipping in and out of consciousness. At Nashville, the surgeon carefully pulled the musket ball from three inches deep, stopping the gushing blood and binding the wound carefully. Amazingly, the resilient hero survived this traumatic third injury, though he lost the sight in his left eye.

When he had recovered enough for travel, he was sent back to New Haven to train the latest conscripts. Here he married Mary Louise Lacey on November 16, 1864. Meanwhile, the war went well for the Union. The Twentieth continued on Sherman's famous March to the Sea. The men encountered former slaves who expressed "frantic joy at the sight of the 'old flag,' which they would caressingly embrace." These newly freed Americans had a reason to be proud. After a string of other battles, James Jackson and the rest of the African American soldiers of the Connecticut Twenty-ninth were the first Union infantry to enter the fallen Confederate capital of Richmond, driving out snipers and skirmishers. President Lincoln followed later that day, and the exhausted troops cheered their leader and the end of the war.

On May 20, 1865, the Whitney Rifles arrived in Washington, D.C., to take part in the great review by president and cabinet. With a patch on his eye, the recently promoted Major Ezra Day Dickerman joined his men before they all took the railroad back to New Haven. At last, the Hamden men of Dickerman's company could walk wearily to their homes, having fought under nearly every general in the Union. Like so many others, Ezra had found the courage to serve, but he returned to a changed Hamden. Eli Whitney's grandnephew Edward Blake had been targeted as an officer at Cedar Mountain and killed. Mrs. Clarence E. Shepard sadly reported, "My mother's brother…starved to death in prison. Although they sent him food, he never received it. At least some other starving person received it. At least it helped someone, either enemy or not." There were empty seats in church pews and missing voices at Bellamy's Tavern.

Still, victories lived among the sorrows. Always a center of industry, Hamden welcomed hundreds of settlers to work in new factories spurred on by the war. Veterans prospered, such as Benjamin Woodin, who lost an arm but survived to plant a dozen orchards and serve as a state representative. Nurses like Sylvia Doolittle and Sarah Chadwick opened a national dialogue on the place of women in society. And when the remaining African American troops of the Twenty-ninth finally reached Hartford, they marched under a huge banner listing their battles. A party waited for them at city hall, thrown by citizens grateful for these soldiers' service. They had lost a shocking 470 men from the regiment but gained the respect of a nation. This new feeling was obvious shortly afterward at Lincoln's funeral, when former slave William Singleton commanded sixty of his troops in the procession. After the war, he moved north to Hamden and finally had the time to learn to read. It took this extraordinary American only one month to do so.

William Peck of Hamden had been at West Point when the war began and served as part of the regular army. In his *West Point Diary*, he summed up the feeling of the town and the Union in 1867:

> *Our country has been rudely tried and its republican form of government has been severely tested. Armies of unequal numbers, skill, and courage have been hurled against each other led by my friends, my boy companions, or the acquaintances of my early years. Blood has flowed like river torrents and land has mourned. As the surgeon cuts deep into the quivering flesh of the patient to extirpate the deeply rooted cancer that is eating away his life, so has God laid bare the nerves of this great nation that He might root out and extirpate the great cancer of slavery. The throbs and agonies of the*

The grave of Ezra Day Dickerman in Centerville stands in front of the tall monument to his three tragic sisters. *Courtesy of the author.*

great struggle have hardly ceased to agitate the body politic, but it may be seen by any who would read and learn that we are about to become a new and I hope a better people.

After the war, Ezra, his young wife Mary and their first child moved halfway between Hamden and Bridgeport to West Haven, eager to begin a new life. But although he was praised as a "man and soldier of more than ordinary worth and ability," he was finally only human. The terrible head wound from Peach Tree Creek did not improve, and he struggled with migraines. Ezra's second child greeted the world in November 1867 but never had the chance to know his father. A mere month later, in a fit of agonizing pain, the brave veteran succumbed to the abscess forming deep in his skull. His service had ended too soon. In her grief, Mary named the boy Ezra after his heroic father, and we can only hope that the child gave her some solace, perhaps sweetening one of the many bitter tragedies of the American Civil War.

CHAPTER 6

Axles and Brass

W hen the eleventh of Elam Ives's children was born in 1815, he decided to name the boy after his hardworking father, who on his deathbed had uttered, "Well, Elam, the sun has got up before me this morning, which it has not done before in twenty years." Thus, little James Ives had a lot to live up to. His father, Elam, was no slouch either. He had fought in the Revolutionary War at age sixteen, purchased a four-acre lot by the Mill River a year after Hamden was founded, built a nine-room house with a huge center chimney and tilled a thriving farm. He also married Sarah Hitchcock and raised a huge family, taking them to weekly services at the Mount Carmel Congregational Church. During the dark years of the War of 1812, Elam saw an opportunity and established a freight line from Boston to New York to avoid the British naval blockade. With two wagons drawn by two yokes of oxen and a horse, James's older brothers carried on the only regular cargo service between the two cities during the entire war.

However, the Ives family's destiny truly changed when the Farmington Canal was dredged directly through their property. Like many in the area, Elam helped to build sections of it and lost a lot of money when it failed. Unlike some of his neighbors, he decided to ignore his losses and use the power of the water to try his hand at another business. He helped his older sons open a factory in 1833 called the Axle Works. New Haven was the number one city in the United States for manufacturing carriages, so it seemed a natural business to invest in. However, at the time, foreign goods were much more prevalent and enriched many American importers, who unfortunately saw this new American business as cutting into easy profits. As

Built in 1790 by Elam Ives, this house was the birthplace of his son James and still stands today. *Courtesy of the Hamden Historical Society.*

James later said proudly, "This, without question, was the first development in America of making iron carriage axles by machinery: using the engine lathe and boring machine, for turning and fitting the arm and box of the axle." It was also the first time anyone had used iron to craft the entire axle. They competed with those who still made cheaper wooden axles, but brother Henry turned out to be a savvy salesman, trading these new iron axles up and down the seaboard.

The Ives family had begun to transform Mount Carmel from a sleepy backwater village into a vital part of Hamden's industrial revolution. Little James was a generation younger than his brothers but wanted to contribute. He found his opportunity when a man named Willis Churchill traveled into Mount Carmel to manufacture brass augers and boring tools, primarily used for surgery. At the time, Churchill was the only one in the United States doing so. At age seventeen, James apprenticed himself to this entrepreneur to learn founding and metalwork, working for only eight dollars per month. Eventually, Churchill moved his factory to the Mill River south of Centerville, where another small village center sprang up around it. Known as Augerville, it straddled the line with North Haven and was considered a separate neighborhood of Hamden until the twentieth century.

Churchill gave James knowledge of mechanics and metalwork second to none. At only twenty years old, the youngest Ives built a small brass foundry in his brothers' factory. He imported copper from the West Indies and began making other carriage parts from brass, such as hubs to cap the end of his brothers' iron axles. A fire had destroyed a nearby mill, and he snatched up this valuable land, calling his new enterprise James Ives and Company. Then, in 1842, James moved the business across the Mill River, taking over a factory built seven years earlier on a dirt road off of Whitney Avenue, a mile and a half south of the Axle Works at the Sleeping Giant. It also happened to be less than one hundred yards from his parents' house.

The previous owners, Edwin Buddington and Judah Frisbie, had used the building to make carriage springs in the Jonathan Mix style. They had likely been run out of business by town notable Charles Brockett, who now ran another spring factory near the Axle Works north of the Steps. Like his second cousin, sculptor Chauncey Ives, James had some artistic talent, creating his own patterns for the brass hardware on both carriages and harnesses. He then expanded his business and sold his first big shipments to wealthy New Yorkers who were sick of the current English style. His new pieces were also lighter, and his hubcaps quickly became in vogue throughout the city. His older brother, Lucius Ives, carted the coal from the dock to the factory for a dollar per ton, making two trips of two tons each day on dirt roads. On his way down to the docks, he took loads of Ives brass products to the steamboats. Fighting against nationwide recessions, James was now in a position to make Mount Carmel a force in industry.

Of course, Hamden already had a booming industrial village at its far end—Whitneyville. After Eli Whitney died in 1825, his nephews Eli and Philos Blake had taken control of the armory. In 1833, President Andrew Jackson rode his white horse up the old Cheshire Turnpike to see whether they were measuring up to Whitney's level of excellence. The famously prickly Jackson inspected the factory, but instead of criticism, he found much to admire. After the Blakes left to start their own business, trustees managed the armory until 1842, when Eli Whitney's only son came of age and took control. The factory had fallen quite a ways in those seven years, and Whitney's original machinery looked worn and shabby, not to mention hopelessly out of date. Eli Whitney Jr. set about fixing the water wheels and seeking out new contracts. He made the Harpers Ferry rifle for the government, the first percussion lock rifle ever made in the country. He experimented with steel rifle barrels, using a mild, softer metal and naming it decarbonized steel. He refitted the drilling machines at the factory so that both the metal rod and the drill revolved, forming a cleaner and straighter barrel. The process was copied throughout the United States. Colonel Jefferson Davis, later leader of the Confederacy, told Whitney Jr. personally that they were the best rifles he had ever fired.

In 1847, an inventor and entrepreneur named Samuel Colt came to Hamden to persuade the second Whitney to craft revolvers for him. The model was the Whitney-Walker Colt, later considered the rarest and most valuable of Colt's countless firearms. This success rescued Colt from financial disaster and spurred him to build his own arms company in Hartford. Whitney Jr. took many other contracts, from both domestic and foreign interests. He replaced the iron barrels of guns with steel, and his rifles were called "the finest" during the Mexican War. Kit Carson said that his Whitney rifle was "just the thing for those setting out to cross the plains." By 1852, the armory had five hundred employees, and Whitney continued to improve breech-loading and magazine rifles, putting his own stamp on the work that his father had begun.

Centerville industry flourished as well. A relation of the Hamden Goodyears named Charles had found a way of taking the sticky, tacky substance from rubber trees and turning it into something practical. In nearby New Haven, he stirred, boiled and kneaded, stinking of the raw, sickly sweet odor wherever he went. However, Hamden entrepreneur Leverett Candee was not put off by Goodyear's stench and saw his genius instead. The failed book-paper manufacturer decided to use this "vulcanization" and bought a license to make rubber shoes and flexible suspenders at a factory in Centerville. He improved the product further, developing the modern elastic material used for these canvas and rubber shoes. In the 1840s, Candee baked thousands of "croquet sandals" a day.

Goodyear himself often traveled to Hamden to oversee the process, and later Candee brought in inventor Nathaniel Hayward to improve the business. Sixteen-year-old Mary Jane Beecher began work in 1843 at Candee's factory, the Centerville Rubber Shoe Shop. She lived in a boardinghouse owned by the company and, as she said, "All we had to do was to make one set of shoes each day." By the 1850s, over 150 people like Mary worked at the Candee factory, the first in the world to manufacture what would later be called sneakers.

When the railroad took over the canal right of way in 1845, angry farmers forced the abandonment of the canal factories. This setback forced Henry Ives to buy the Munson mill site, which Albert Goodyear had been using to craft spokes. In 1853, Henry Ives and Charles Brockett made deals with the railroad and water companies and were able to divert water through the

The Upper Shop at the Mount Carmel Axle Works rose high above the canal and utilized the old Munson Dam. *Courtesy of the Hamden Historical Society.*

old canal to power their factory. They now owned all of the land between Whitney Avenue and the Mill Pond north of the Steps, and they built a second factory and improved the old Munson one. The ingenious way they brought water from a nearby brook allowed the water to be used twice, once for the upper factory along Whitney and once for the lower one where Munson's stood. The new railroad provided a perfect tool for bringing in raw materials and sending back finished axles.

Though Henry Ives owned the Axle Works, he lived in a big house in New Haven, spending his energy and time in the various clubs and societies available there. He had followed the dream of many, which was to make enough money to leave the small town where he was born. James had a different dream. When he met Lucy Ann Candee of Oxford, he brought her to Hamden, and they never left, happy in their new house down the road from the factory. We can assume that Lucy found joy in her husband's large, intense eyes and understood that his ambition had physical boundaries. After all, James always said that he wanted Hamden to be an "independent industrial community." To brother Henry, now steeped in the advantages and society of New Haven, this must have seemed quaint. However, James set his thin upper lip and forged on.

To help local businesses become financially stable, James started a bank and building association, bought the local water company and dammed the Mill River in two places to make Clark's Pond and Ives's Pond. He built

James Ives's nonstop commitment to local business helped make Hamden successful in the nineteenth century. *Courtesy of the Hamden Historical Society.*

a brick building on Whitney Avenue and rented it out as a general store. In 1853, James partnered yet again, this time with E.S. Pierce. Pierce had invented machinery for making wood screws and wanted Ives's expertise to make the business happen. Eventually, James took over as the owner and organized the Mount Carmel Screw Works as a stock company. The Churchill factory in Centerville was taken over by the Ives family in the 1850s as well and was reorganized as the Hamden Auger Company. James was also finding himself busy as the father of five daughters: Catherine, Lucy, Mary, Sarah and Helen.

In 1855, the factory on Ives Street became the Ives, Pardee Manufacturing Company. It sold stocks, and James came out of the deal with $25,000. Now the president rather than owner, James noted proudly that he "purchased a small malleable iron works and erected a brass foundry containing twelve furnaces." The town paved a public road called Broadway to connect this larger brick building to Ridge Road and the Hartford Turnpike, though it later charged the company for the work. Although James was still president of the company, the new board of directors from New Haven and New York began to abuse its privileges, placing friends and supporters in positions of power. The stockholders lost their money, and after five years the joint stock company went bankrupt, having lost over $60,000, a fortune at the time. James had been able to do nothing about this tragedy, suffering while others damaged his livelihood and his town. With characteristic fortitude, he partnered with J.A. Granniss and bought back the dying company. They agreed to never give a business note and worked to redeem the hard-won reputation lost so quickly by the greed and shortsightedness of the directors.

By now, a variety of local industries were well established. Seeing opportunity during an oil shortage, a laborer named William D. Hall started a business in the far northeast of the town, bringing in tons of Menhaden fish. He used an ingenious steam tank process to render out their valuable oils, selling them for a profit. But then, Hall found something even more useful. Without its oils, the fish scrap could be used as fertilizer. This was a radical idea and practice at the time and, in time, greatly increased the nutrition of New England's failing soil. But Hall wasn't the only local with a mind ripe for invention. In 1859, Reverend Everest of the Rectory School approached a Centerville storekeeper named John Henry. Everest scolded Henry for not carrying a better pair of shears at his store. Henry replied that there were no better shears available. After reflection on the problem, Henry invented a new type of pruning shears with a curved blade that snapped against a curved jaw. He promptly manufactured them, and they began selling to Australia, Europe and South America.

In 1863, the former Candee Factory on the Mill River in Centerville was occupied by Bela Mann, Ward Coe and Joseph Leavenworth, who opened the New Haven Web Company. Mann had invented a strange new loom to make elastic and non-elastic webbing of different sorts and created patterns of webbing previously never seen. By 1866, they had enough money to buy the factory outright and continued to expand their business. A fire in 1875 destroyed all of the old buildings, but the Web Company quickly rebuilt a huge brick structure, to which it continued to add as success followed success. By 1886, it occupied a 245-foot-long factory, an enormous storeroom half its size, a water-wheel building, a dyeing building, stables, sheds and thirteen houses and apartments. Approximately 105 of Mann's looms took up the factory floor, and 125 people were employed in the business, including a professional pattern designer. Companies in New York and beyond bought this webbing, which was often decorated with colored silk, for use in products like suspenders, shoes and underwear.

Dozens of smaller businesses dotted the new industrial landscape as well. Since 1841, Franklin Hall had run a popular silver smithy in Centerville, while W.F. Gibbs made organ stop knobs. In 1863, ice-cutting operations

The Ives factory stood on the banks of the Mill River, turning out brass carriage hardware. Its success allowed James Ives to expand Mount Carmel's industry. *Courtesy of the Hamden Historical Society.*

began to provide blocks for New Haven County from the many ponds and lakes. In the 1870s, stockyards in Hamden Plains and the State Street area found success. With no previous experience, R.S. Clark started a company in 1875 to make silk. By 1886, he was doing well, and his son, Herman, patented a process to cover cotton thread with silk. Inventor William Witte brought his Paper Box Works out of New Haven to Hamden, selling his strawboard boxes to all of the local manufacturers, making him a necessary and popular man in the booming factory town.

James Ives must have looked proudly on both of these developments and his own accomplishments. After nine years of hard work, he had brought the brass foundries at Ives and Granniss back to their previous reputations and profitability. His other businesses were flourishing, and he had a rich family life. The Mount Carmel Female Seminary, which Ives had helped the Dickerman sisters found, had, after their deaths, become the Academy Hall for the local school district. However, in the 1860s the town built a larger school, and James Ives moved into the old seminary on Murlyn Road, adding an Italianate porch and center gable. High up the hill on the west side of the Cheshire Turnpike, James could see the hills of the Sleeping Giant above and the small industrial village he had built below.

James's older brother Henry had died, and his nephew Frederick took over the Axle Works, winning praise from his uncle: "His superior judgment and watchful care were ever manifest in the essentials of a business where life and limb are dependent upon the quality of material and workmanship." Meanwhile, James's partner, Granniss, had also opened the Carriage Pole Works, which used Ives's patented pole and had become the most popular maker of carriage poles in the United States, shipping them from Maine to Georgia. However, now Granniss was getting on in years and sold his interest in the Brass Works to W.W. Woodruff. Woodruff managed the sales and office, and Ives continued to spearhead the manufacturing end of the business. He was no longer young himself but continued to try to meet the demands of increased orders of their loyal customers. During the nine years after the bankruptcy, they had barely spent any money on travel and none on advertising, relying completely on the quality of their products. Woodruff increased this already prosperous company by using his own contacts in the business world, and James continued his brothers' work to improve axles and self-adjusting harnesses, as well as patenting a glass water pipe, an air pump condenser and a glass hydraulic ram.

Others had also found success by following the Ives family's lead, such as Lyman Todd, who apprenticed with James and later founded the hugely successful Union Brass Company of Chicago. But the story of Willis Miller was particularly illuminating. As scarcely more than a boy, Willis Miller began his career as a hammersman's helper in the Axle Works, with no other education than that received in the one-room schoolhouse on the hill. Slowly but surely he rose through the ranks in the Ives factory, found love and married a local girl named Mary Bradley. Eventually, he invented a patent axle that "bore his name." Partnering with James's nephew, Frederick, Willis Miller continued to manufacture all sorts of axles for carriages and wagons. Finally, when Frederick retired, Willis bought and renamed Ives, Miller and Company. Along with holding a number of important positions in New Haven, this hardworking American eventually became the president of every single manufactory in Mount Carmel, except the Clark silk mill.

This was exactly what James Ives had hoped to inspire, a combination of loyalty, hard work and innovation in which individual success is linked to the local community. In his old age, Ives himself continued to begin new projects, becoming president of the new Mount Carmel Bolt Company in 1880, crafting stove bolts, tire bolts and rivets. The master mechanic at the company, Edward McLane, invented automatic machines that made "cold-pressed swedged nuts" for tire bolts. James generally allowed this local inventor the run of his factory floor, knowing that such talent should be nurtured.

In 1863, the old Candee Rubber Factory on Whitney Avenue became the New Haven Web Company, one of Hamden's most successful businesses. *Courtesy of the Hamden Historical Society.*

Finally, in 1883 Ives decided that fifty years of constant creative management was enough and retired. A freight schooner out of West Haven was named in his honor. He sold his factories to Willis Miller, who continued to prosper, dominating the carriage industry until the automobile put it out of business. As for James, he could watch things from his house on the hill and walk through the independent industrial town that was his dream. When he died, he donated his home, the old female seminary, to be the Mount Carmel Children's Home for orphans. He had truly "spent his fortune as accumulated, in his native parish of Mount Carmel." No doubt every town has a rock whose ripples do not reach outside the pond but whose impact within is incalculable. For Hamden, James Ives was such a rock, and his belief that individual success should be tied to the community in which it thrives continues to ripple through America today.

CHAPTER 7

The Labor of His Days

From the gray porch of Appledore, William James Linton could see across the Quinnipiac River to the hills of North Haven. Behind the low-roofed home, fields of sunflowers and honeysuckle rose to the craggy hill of East Rock, now a popular picnic spot on lazy Sundays. Occasionally, the pokeweed along dusty State Street would be disturbed by a produce wagon or the Wallingford stagecoach. It seemed a fine and anonymous place for a busy person to retire. Linton's neighbors were probably unaware that this bearded, affable old man was an infamous revolutionary, friends with some of the most famous people in the world and known throughout Europe and America as a poet, essayist, politician, editor, translator, printer, publisher, artist and engraver.

William Linton was born in London in 1812 in a lower-class neighborhood and spent his childhood pushing vainly against the poverty caused by England's class system. Finding early on that he had artistic talent, he apprenticed to the best of England's engravers and became a critical and financial success. This gave him the independence from his own poverty, but for this committed man, that wasn't enough. Linton saw no reason why the majority of people should have their freedom curtailed simply because a privileged few made the rules. He spent his time championing liberal republicanism in England, as well as the independence of countries like Poland and Italy. With journals and pamphlets, he promoted free speech, freedom of the press and suffrage for women and minorities.

With his bright blue eyes, long fair hair and a heavy beard, Linton made an immediate impression. His clothes were "out of fashion" and eccentric,

Already haunted by injustice as a young man, William Linton fought bitterly for the rights of the oppressed. *Courtesy of Magnus Wahlstrom Library, University of Bridgeport.*

including antique trousers, a broad-brimmed black hat and Wellington boots. He wore turndown collars when everyone else turned them up. Full of energy, he walked in a "breezy rush," moving from labor to labor with a determined will. This energetic man found a job engraving for the largest and most significant periodical in the world, the *London Illustrated News*. He married, but after only a year his wife died. Ever unconventional, he married her sister, and both found solace in each other after their mutual loss.

At age forty, Linton moved to Coniston, in England's Lake District. His second wife died, and he married again, to Eliza Lynn, a popular author. The matrimony only lasted a few years, but she continued to raise his two daughters from the previous marriage. Here in the picturesque hills and vales of the Lake District, he published more tracts and books on the necessity of universal suffrage, becoming entangled in the politics of the Chartist movement. Many of the so-called Chartists were sent to penal colonies in Australia. William probably only escaped arrest due to his fame as an engraver and his friends in the literary world—like Dante G. Rossetti, Thomas Carlyle, William Thackeray and Robert Browning. Still, things became uncomfortable for Linton, and he sold his Lake District house to friend and famous philosopher John Ruskin.

By the time he set foot in America, he was exhausted. His third marriage was failing, and his many contributions to political causes had put him in debt. Though he originally came to America in part to win support for the Italian revolutionary movement, he decided that he needed a break. Although there was a long way to go in 1870, the progress for workers' rights he saw in America probably compared favorably to Britain. However, New York City did not feel right to the fifty-eight-year-old Linton, and he thought about returning to England when a friend named William John Hennessey invited him to Hamden.

Hennessey was an Irish-born artist whose striking paintings of simple folk in action had won him a place at the National Academy of Design. Like Linton, he had been involved in a revolutionary movement and had been forced to flee Ireland. He stayed in Hamden while engaged in work in New Haven and met Linton through mutual friends. Having established himself as a reputable artist at the young age of thirty-one, Hennessey was planning to move back across the Atlantic to England, where he could find a better audience for his delicate figures and luminous landscapes. The Irish artist offered his small 1795 house on State Street to Linton, who took it eagerly.

Linton named the house Appledore for the orchard that spread out in his backyard toward the abrupt rise of the East Rock. It must have seemed a little like the English Lake District he had left. He brought his ink-stained desk, "servant, companion, and friend for more than half a century," from England and set it on the ground floor, facing north. A large fireplace warmed him nearly as much as his treasured books, which were piled high along walls and on chairs. Photographs of his heroes and small paintings, such as a riverscape by James Whistler, crowded onto the walls. He could glance out the dormer windows to watch people netting pigeons in the Quinnipiac salt meadows. But Linton would not be alone in his retirement.

Before Linton left England, he and his wife separated cordially and corresponded. However, his son and daughters joined him at Appledore. His daughter Ellen was twenty-three in 1875. She helped him research, copy and set type on an old-fashioned press. His son, Edmund, was little better than an invalid, and his other daughter lay paralyzed in an asylum until the end of the 1870s, when she died. His last daughter, Margaret, married a Yale professor, Thomas Mather. Though Ellen helped take care of her aging father, the Lintons also employed a housekeeper, Mrs. Moss, who baked them rich Yorkshire puddings. William threw a huge Christmas party every year for this transplanted family and their friends, entertaining everyone with his stories, dry laughs and merry songs.

William Linton bought this 1785 house and named it Appledore. It remains standing in the shadow of East Rock today. *Courtesy of Amy Nawrocki.*

Hamden was already well known as a place to retire. Born in Connecticut, James J. Webb spent his years in New Mexico as a Santa Fe trader. On August 1, 1857, he left Santa Fe for Hamden, rich and nearly ready to settle down at only thirty-nine years old. He bought the farmland owned by the West Indies sugar barons the Van den Heuvals between Whitneyville and Centerville. Moving in with his wife and son, he became involved with civil service, serving as selectman and state senator. Webb named his extensive dairy farm on both sides of Whitney Avenue Spring Glen and experimented on this land, trying different types of fertilizers. He became the president of the New Haven County Agricultural Society and the Farmer's Club. Running the huge experimental farm occupied his time, with its eight hundred chickens and one hundred Holstein cows, which produced the "ideal nursery food," Spring Glen milk. Webb's farm was also the first to introduce lactonic buttermilk in the area. He wrote to his business partner, "Spring has come, and I am very busy farming and you must excuse any brevity or irregularity in my letters, as I am now a working man, and I get pretty tired by nights, and my hand is stiff days." Never slowing down, he organized the Agricultural Experiment Station and wrote a memoir of his days as a trader.

Like Webb, William Linton's ideas of retirement had nothing to do with relaxation. For the last twenty-seven years of his life, for ten hours a day, seven days a week, he worked at painting, writing, engraving or printing. He gardened for vegetables, wrote and engraved, using the heavy press. Though not deep in the city, his property was not quite the pastoral idyll that the northern reaches of Hamden were. A few hundred yards down State Street an enormous brick-making operation had been going on since the 1600s, with millions of bricks baked every year. Linton was near the center of action and could walk around the bluff of East Rock into New Haven quite easily. He often walked the city streets to study at the Yale Library, designed decades earlier by Henry Austin. There, if he wished, he could read the latest newspapers from London and curse what he saw as the continued oppression of the poor.

Linton's Hamden neighbors were probably unaware of his revolutionary past, although it is doubtful that they would have cared. There were already plenty of eccentrics in town, like Dr. Daniel Hurd, a former slave from Virginia who ran a business as a healer in the Highwood area. Hurd wore a silk hat and Prince Albert coat with dark, striped trousers and high gumboots and carried no medical degree. There must have been something appealing about this "doctor," however. People came from as far as West Haven to be treated and swore by his strange cures and therapies. The "Leatherman" was a frequent visitor to Hamden, as well, staying in a small cave on the top of High Rock once every thirty-four days. This mysterious character tramped a circuit around Connecticut and New York, dressed in a patched leather outfit, refusing to settle down or to sleep indoors.

Independent characters like the Leatherman and William Linton found sympathy in this town of pioneers. In fact, Hamden had previously received European radicals with open arms. In April 1852, Hungarian patriot Louis Kossuth visited the gun factory in Whitneyville, receiving twenty-five rifles as a gift in support of his country's independence. In earlier years, Linton had actually corresponded with Kossuth. He also remained friends with Italian revolutionary patriots Giuseppe Mazzini and Garibaldi, whom he had helped find support in France. The European revolutionary Admiral de Rohan actually visited him at Appledore. However, though Linton sometimes pursued his goals of equality through his press, he stayed out of American politics and was able to put the "intolerable" situation in Britain behind him.

Instead, Linton turned to literature as his primary interest in middle and old age. He stopped sending letters to the editor, a nearly constant habit before he came to Hamden. His reputation as an engraver had preceded him to America, and he was immediately given plenty of well-paying artistic work for a variety of books and journals. He corresponded with John Greenleaf Whittier, of whom he would later write a biography. He visited American literary icon Walt Whitman and befriended Julia Ward Howe, author of

"The Battle Hymn of the Republic." He dined with Ralph Waldo Emerson in Concord. Linton found much to admire in his adopted country, and in 1878 he published *Poetry of America*, considered the first solid anthology of American verse. Walt Whitman himself called it "a capital compilation and condensation." It was also the first collection to include "the hymns and song of the slaves." Linton also published the five-volume set of *English Verse*, introducing Americans to the poetry from his native land.

Linton did not neglect his own literary work, either. He contributed to magazines with essays, stories and reviews. He wrote poetry of his own, like "Unseen Worth," which read:

> *A single drop of rain fell from the skies:*
> *None saw it, on that day so bright and fair.*
> *It slid into the ground, and nourish'd there*
> *The acorn of an oak to live for centuries.*

He published books of his cavalier poems, like *Love Lore*, at the age of seventy, turning to traditional poetic themes of flowers, wine and romance. He wrote and illustrated books as diverse as *Stories for Children*, a book of imaginary plays called *Windfalls*, a biography of an English political activist named James Watson and *Practical Hints on Wood Engraving*, a small volume immediately considered a standard resource in the field.

Of course, he was only one of many Hamden artists and writers. The younger brother of Ezra Day Dickerman, George Sherwood, had become a pastor in New Haven, but his heart never left Hamden. This became clear when he wrote *The Old Mount Carmel Parish: Origins and Outgrowths*. From another branch of the family, Carolyn Dickerman wrote poems, one of which, "The Northern Mount," celebrated her home by the Sleeping Giant:

> *And the dear old house is abiding still*
> *By the northern mount and the western hill*
> *Where the sun sinks nightly to his rest*
> *On his daily round from east to west.*

The grandson of Captain Jonathan Mix, William P. Blake, became a mineralogist and geologist, surveyed the railroad route to the Pacific, found an ancient turquoise mine in New Mexico and discovered the Stickeen glacier. The United States bought Alaska from Russia largely on the strength of his surveys. He moved to Mill Rock on Deepwood Drive,

This Linton engraving of pioneers in the American West could have taken place in Hamden one hundred years earlier. *Courtesy of Magnus Wahlstrom Library, University of Bridgeport.*

wrote many books on geology and completed the *History of the Town of Hamden, Connecticut.*

It was not only writers who found inspiration here. There were painters like George Henry Durrie, a landscape artist with Currier and Ives who painted many scenes of rural Hamden in the late nineteenth century, including East and West Rock. And there were musicians like J. Burns Moore, who started playing homemade drums at age ten in his Highwood home. After being inspired by the Governor's Foot Guard Band at the Whitney Armory, Burns began serious study under New Haven expert Jack Lyneham, and by age nineteen he was performing at the local theatres. He took Lyneham's place in the Governor's Foot Guard and later joined the New Haven Symphony, going undefeated in individual drumming contests throughout the 1890s. Later, he became the president of the National Association of Rudimental Drummers and wrote a method book called *The Art of Drumming.*

Linton found joy and fulfillment in literature, but his real expertise was wood engraving. Though his politics were ahead of their time, he was a conservative when it came to etching and often raged against the "new school" of artists who depended on photography and violated the conventions of line engraving. He felt that the new engravers were becoming mere copiers of art rather than interpreters and artists in their own right. Though many younger artists scoffed at his "ancient" ideas, he was so trusted in the field that the British Museum lent him prints to write his book *Masters of Wood Engraving*. This combination of history and aesthetic theory was praised by the *Nation*, the *Saturday Review* and the *Atlantic Monthly*, which called it "a labor of love." A demonstration of both technical skill and intimate knowledge, it became an instant classic even though only four initial copies were printed. Yale University honored Linton with a master's degree on the strength of this work. Linton said, "Let the engraver, then, doubt nothing so much as praise for mere mechanical success. Let him study, even in his most obedient work, to be a true and uncompromising artist." A London publishing house printed six hundred copies, and in 1882 he was elected to the American National Academy of the Arts, the first wood engraver to be so honored. Many publications, including *Encyclopedia Britannica*, considered Linton to be the best engraver of the age.

By the mid-1880s, Linton had established himself as an editor, writer and engraving artist. Along with this creative work, he printed a new book every month under the imprint of Appledore Press. The old "Hoe hand" press was already a relic when he used it, but it served him well, allowing him to publish small runs of his own work, as well as Christmas cards, children's poems and broadsides. Often, he would send copies of these beautiful tomes to larger publishers, who were intimidated by the quality of the edition but attempted to duplicate it. Not surprisingly, Linton was not the only printer in Hamden. William Baldwin Beemish ran a shop on Whitney Avenue, or so everyone thought. It turned out that he had died many years before and his wife had assumed his identity, living as a man for forty years. Of course, Mrs. Beemish was not quite in the same league as William Linton, who is often credited with starting the small press movement in America.

The blizzard of 1888, which isolated and buried houses in fifteen-foot drifts, did not stop Linton's work. New houses sprang up across the road, ruining his view, and a regular train whistled past at all hours. However, Linton had retreated, or perhaps advanced, into a "private invulnerable innocence." He had found peace, not in rural idyll, but in working his hot printing press every day. On his eighty-fifth birthday, the Century Club gave him a special dinner in New York. He wrote a memoir of his friendships with both famous and infamous people. However, he caught pneumonia and, by 1897, could no longer use the hand press. His loyal grandsons attempted to help him finish a last volume of poems in 1898, but his faithful housekeeper Mrs. Moss died, and Linton passed shortly thereafter in December.

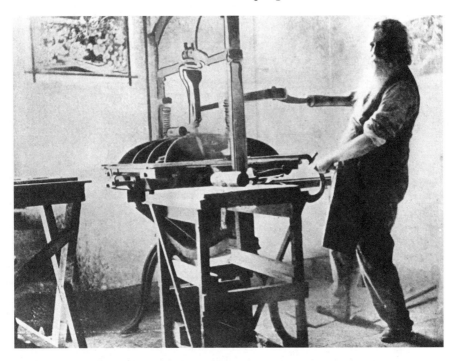

As an old man, Linton continued to work his heavy printing press every day, churning out poetry, political pamphlets and children's books. *Courtesy of the Hamden Historical Society.*

One of several self-written epitaphs reads:

Though I myself may all forgotten die,
What I have rightly done or said will live.
My friends: the perishing ill in me forgive
And hold the better part in memory.

He was right about what he had "rightly done or said" living on. Eventually, the ability to use actual photographs would invalidate the practice of wood engraving for books and thus validate Linton's theory of engraving as a necessarily separate art. His political goals began to be realized all around the world during the twentieth century, and over the next one hundred years, many rights that he fought for would come to pass. Radical notions like equality for all would become nearly universal. As far as his "perishing ill," we can only fault an idealistic compassion and perhaps a tendency to overwork. However, if not for this constant, creative work, William Linton would not have found the peace he sought—the profound and satisfying labor of his days.

CHAPTER 8

Building Suburbia

When Alice Washburn and her husband drove their new "automobile" through Hamden during the early twentieth century, they found a land of contrasts. Modern factory housing and industry clustered in the town centers, with small farms and mills on the outskirts. In Mount Carmel, dirt roads split off from the main artery of Whitney Avenue. Horse and surrey were still used by many inhabitants, and children walked to one-room schoolhouses. Gentleman tramps, sons of the Leatherman, walked the back roads and slept in the gooseberry bushes of West Woods. Doctors still made house calls, and home dentistry was practiced by many. Daily newspapers arrived a day late, and families still lived in houses they had built with their own hands along the foot of West Rock or Sleeping Giant, keeping beehives, apple trees and chicken coops.

There were changes, of course. Whitney's grandson had sold the armory to Winchester Repeating Arms in 1888. At the other end of town, the town's birthplace, Bellamy's Tavern, had fallen to development in 1880, when a feed store replaced it, and the Upper Axle Works burned a few decades later. Though watering troughs were still available for horses on the main thoroughfares, Dixwell, Circular and the southern part of Whitney Avenue had been paved at the turn of the century. Babcock Hill in Whitneyville and parts of the Hartford Turnpike were leveled. Gaslights and hydrants were commonplace. The trolley line stretched from New Haven to Centerville and then expanded north to Mount Carmel in 1903, putting an end to railroad passenger service.

But with Alice Washburn and the arrival of American suburbia, this landscape would change nearly beyond recognition. Born Alice Trythall

Whitney Avenue in the late nineteenth century still appeared rustic and undeveloped, despite the railroad paralleling it. *Courtesy of the Hamden Historical Society.*

in nearby Cheshire in 1870, she attended finishing school and became a schoolteacher in Springfield, Massachusetts. By her mid-twenties she had earned the job of school principal and met Edward Washburn, a wallpaper manufacturer. She raised two daughters, Martha and Frances, and came back to Cheshire in 1909. Like Alice, many women born nearby in nineteenth-century Hamden had gone into the field of education. Sue Dickerman taught from the end of the Civil War until 1915, an unbroken fifty years of teaching Hamden children. Mrs. Tuttle brought the first traveling library to town, and two years later, Mrs. Brewster founded the Mount Carmel Free Public Library. Florence Peck established a private school at Hillfield Farm in West Woods in 1915. By 1918, Emma Dickerman was running a private school for youngsters at her house on Whitney Avenue, echoing the three Dickerman sisters of long ago. Alice Washburn had followed that tradition as well. But then, in 1919, after two other careers and before she even had the right to vote, she filed her first building permit.

At the time, less than 1 percent of American architects were women. It was difficult to get into architecture school and even more difficult to apprentice at a firm. No one knows what made Alice Washburn decide to begin this profession at age forty-nine. Her granddaughter said that Alice believed that since "society had placed women in charge of domestic affairs, they were uniquely qualified to design houses." So, with no formal training, she decided to use the money she had inherited from her parents to buy lots in Hamden on speculation and began drawing up plans.

Though her first houses were similar to the new Colonials then in style throughout the country, she immediately changed small details. Even those first attempts were meticulously and impeccably designed, with personal touches that matched her refined personality. Washburn's landlady in later years said that "by seven thirty in the morning she would be dressed in a black dress with pearls or velvet ribbon." She kept a rose in her table vase at all times and was described by her workmen as "very dressy." This sense of simple elegance helped her in her business dealings, of course, but more importantly, it helped her aesthetics. Each house was set in the landscape as if it belonged there. Formal but welcoming entrances and ornamented façades guided guests through elegant dining and living rooms to informal sunrooms or porches. And the landscaping was not ignored, with dogwood, mountain laurel and other native species enhancing walkways and terraces.

Inside, Washburn often settled on a motif, like a scallop shell, and subtly introduced it throughout the house. She also used gables, molding and tracery in unique ways for each house. Her favorite extra was custom millwork, often using mantelpieces as focal points, with elaborate wainscoting and unusual carvings. Valentin Schanz, who ran a millwork shop on State Street in Hamden, contributed to these architectural touches. None of Alice's fireplaces were exactly alike. She also used attached garages, a very unusual luxury at the time. Once she used expensive African mahogany for a library room. And yet, all of these elements fit together in a pleasing and seemingly ordinary way, with no shocking components. Before Washburn, the architecture of Hamden was eclectic to say the least, including standouts like cigar baron Frederick Grave's castle, Lucerne, with its crenellated towers and other medieval follies. But now, a pattern was developing, and Alice

Alice Washburn dressed well for all occasions, even when sitting at her desk to plan new architectural marvels. *Courtesy of the Hamden Historical Society.*

Washburn was developing it. Word-of-mouth recommendations gave her steady business, with more clients than she could possibly serve.

Hamden and North Haven were getting together to plan small communities off the Hartford Turnpike, giving Washburn lots of work on the east side of town. In Whitneyville, Washburn built a high-style Colonial Revival on Mill Rock Road that demonstrated an amazing facility for taking a plain, flush-boarded wall surface and embroidering it with pilasters and other façade details. Another on the Hartford Turnpike used two-story Doric pillars and a denticular cornice. On Swarthmore Street, she used Tuscan columns, a Palladian window and a recessed entryway. Washburn combined elements freely without any attempt to copy historical designs, and yet each unique house stood alone as a model of sophistication.

Many of the homes Washburn built were in the new Spring Glen neighborhood. James J. Webb's name for his farm had stuck, replacing Augerville, and his sons and grandsons decided to parse the land into a new neighborhood. Grandson Arthur Webb entered service in World War I as a pilot. His brother Thomas went into action as a private in all of the major offensives, advanced to the rank of sergeant, fell sick at the Argonne and returned with his brother to develop their grandfather's land. The city helped their project by building Spring Glen School in 1924 and encouraging two clusters of stores within walking distance of all of the houses. Trolleys from New Haven now stopped here at the Glendower Drugstore. People said that the Glen had "no monotony in the landscape" and was the "ideal residential suburb." It would become a model for many city planners throughout the country.

All of Hamden's neighborhoods boomed in the 1920s as new waves of immigrants flowed into the city. Once called Hamburg, the Highwood section of Hamden had been settled early by Germans. They gathered at David Kittler's Eagle Grove Beer Garden and listened to his stories of serving the Union in the Civil War. Later, Jewish immigrants moved in and established Congregation B'nai Shalom, while Irish immigrants arrived to work the railroad and factories. But at the turn of the twentieth century, Italian immigrants became the most numerous, opening stores and taking part in the *fin de siècle* industrial boom. War brought even more settlers. Though African Americans had always been numerous in the south end of Hamden, in 1918 they arrived in large numbers to work at Winchester Repeating Arms. More Italian, German and Irish immigrants poured into Highwood from crowded New Haven. Before 1868, this area had so few people living in it that it was not considered its own neighborhood. By the

By the time Hamden's Memorial Town Hall was built in the 1924, Hamden's main roads had been fully paved. *Courtesy of the Hamden Historical Society.*

end of World War I, it had become the most densely populated of Hamden's districts. John Della Vecchia's store and bakery on St. Mary's Street soon bustled with activity, and nearby Dixwell Avenue became another center of Hamden's commerce.

In Centerville, at the corner where rubber shoe manufacturer Leverett Candee's house once stood, the Memorial Town Hall was erected in 1924, with a series of tributes in the entrance rotunda to Hamden's war heroes. Then, local businessmen decided they needed an independent depository, and Hamden Bank and Trust opened in 1925 on the corner of Circular and Dixwell Avenues in a monumental Neoclassical Revival building. The bank instituted a popular savings program in which even the schoolchildren participated. The Hamden Chamber of Commerce was organized in 1926 to promote the financial interests of the town, and the Hamden Airport sprang up off Dixwell between Morse and Putnam, with service to New York and Hartford.

Farther north up Whitney Avenue, the Connecticut Agricultural Experiment Station, organized by originally by Spring Glen's James J. Webb, may have looked like a farm, but in reality it was pioneering new techniques to feed America. In 1910, Annie McLaughlin sold twenty acres of land on a hill above Whitney Avenue to the station, and in 1917 hybrid corn was developed and grown there. Future vice president of the United States Henry Wallace organized the first company that produced and sold this hybrid corn seed, later saying, "No state Agricultural Experiment Station has even accomplished so much with so little land, money and salaries."

Hamden's services to its citizens also improved. Following Bridgeport's groundbreaking implementation of a dental hygiene regimen for all citizens, Hamden became the first school system in Connecticut to test using fluorine on children's teeth. This led to a quick 40 percent decline in tooth decay. The town also became the first in the state to inoculate children with the Salk polio vaccine. The residents of the rural West Woods area used a subscription to finally gravel and pave the roads so that cars could go over them. The remaining sections of the canal had become stagnant, and mosquitoes were breeding in huge numbers. The town drained it and at the same time began installing modern sanitary sewer systems.

In 1923, the town government decided that random patrols by amateur constables working on a commission basis were no longer enough to keep the peace. They established the Hamden Police Department and hired the first officer, James Whelahan. He and the other early officers drove motorcycles, answered emergency calls from telephone operators and kept prisoners in simple jail cells. Four years later, Whelahan became the first chief of police and later established headquarters in the basement of the new town hall. In 1925, the fire department also became an official branch of government. Hamden's first volunteer fire department had been the Highwood Company, organized in 1896, and it had petitioned successfully for the first hydrants to be installed. The Centerville, Whitneyville, Humphrey and Mount Carmel Companies soon followed, becoming effective forces despite inadequate equipment. The Highwood chief, Charles Loller, became the first chief of Hamden's official fire department, and firefighters like Raymond Spencer took the lead in training the men into an even more professional crew.

Meanwhile, Alice Washburn had also assembled her own crew of outstanding professionals. Her foreman, Hans Iversen, had moved from Denmark to Central Avenue in Spring Glen. Like his employer, he had impeccable taste and understood her style implicitly. Most of the men in her huge workforce were immigrants from Scandinavia, expert craftsmen who enjoyed their jobs and respected Washburn for her consummate professionalism and quest for excellence. When she asked them to soak each wooden shingle in preservative to prevent buckling, they consented readily.

The business was also a family affair. Her daughter Martha had married Charles Farist, an electrical engineer who designed heating and electrical systems for his mother-in-law. Washburn's other daughter, Frances, helped her mother more directly, taking charge of paperwork and chauffeuring Alice to each job in a pickup truck. Eventually, she married Valentin Schanz, the miller who supplied so many excellent mantels, moldings and entrances to these fabulous houses. When Washburn's husband died in 1926, she continued to build. This was her life now. Isabel Wilder, sister of the famous novelist Thornton and owner of a Washburn house, said, "Mrs. Washburn was a busy, professional woman, and we treated her that way, with respect." When asked if they were friends, Wilder laughed at this presumption. "We had lunch several times during the building, of course, but we didn't see her much after the house was built. She was a very busy woman. She wasn't out there playing around, you know."

Having finally won equality in spirit and law with the Nineteenth Amendment, women were now taking a more active role in many areas. They formed the West Woods Circle to sew for the Red Cross and look after the welfare of the whole community. Groups like the Whitneyville Women's Club and the Hamden League of Women Voters also made sure that town affairs were to their satisfaction. Women continued to lead in education as well. Margaret L. Keefe served as the school superintendent of Hamden for an amazing forty-three years, from 1911 to 1954. The cabin of the Rectory School, where C.W. Everest lived, had become the Hamden Public Library at the turn of the century, but in 1924 Mary Miller bequeathed $100,000 in honor of her husband, Willis, to establish a real library with more than just donated books. Her gift would help the town bring its collections together under the auspices of the new Miller Memorial Library and began a tradition of community engagement that women would continue for decades to come.

As one of those women, Alice Washburn was literally building the new Hamden one house at a time. She always operated several projects at once, sometimes with as many as forty carpenters under her supervision. Refusing to compromise quality, she insisted on the best materials and often took a loss to make sure a house was built properly. Once, she tore out a finished bookcase because it didn't meet her standards, even though the owner was satisfied. She also gave her clients good prices, and if she went over budget on a Palladian window or expensive mantelpiece, she simply gave it to the owner for free. This combination of generosity and perfectionism brought her clients and fame, but when the Great Depression hit, Washburn owed $82,000, the equivalent of millions today, and the courts stripped her of everything, including the family homestead in Cheshire. In twelve years, she had built nearly ninety wonderful homes, but now she had none of her own. Moreover, one of the most prolific female architects in the country could no longer practice her art.

The Wall Street crash and following Depression meant more than an end for Alice Washburn's construction projects. A run by scared investors forced

This house on Swarthmore Street in Spring Glen demonstrates Washburn's flair for making the commonplace special. Note how the delightfully dissimilar windows somehow fit together. *Courtesy of the author.*

the Hamden Bank and Trust into receivership. Winchester Repeating Arms went bankrupt, leaving the Whitney factory empty and its testing ground at the Olin Powder Farm an industrial wasteland. The Hamden Airport failed, becoming a barren field used only by Barnum and Bailey's circus. The local *Hamden Times* went under. People sold apples on street corners, and for a few years both businesses and families teetered on the edge of catastrophe.

However, the Depression would not devastate Hamden the way it did many communities in America. The town helped needy families buy fuel, and federal aid money saved many from utter poverty. Three hundred local workers were hired by Roosevelt's Work Projects Administration and given jobs on construction projects. The new Hamden High School was built in 1935, a huge Neoclassical Revival with a Georgian clock tower, the first school to bring all the students of the town together. It helped connect the many villages into one, as children were bused from the outlying areas of the town to the new school. On the sesquicentennial in 1936, the town came together for three days, with parades, pageants, speakers, musicians, exhibits and athletic contests that celebrated its past accomplishments and present happiness.

The Wilbur Cross Parkway was also planned during the Depression, though Hamden would have to wait until after World War II for workers to carve it across town. In 1949, the West Rock Tunnel finally bore through the mountain, allowing motorists to drive from New York to Meriden on the beautiful parkway. Hamden suffered more than many towns when the road was built, essentially being cut across the middle. Many people complained that there were enough problems bringing the separate villages together. Nevertheless, the parkway also brought new life to the town, with exits that steered new drivers directly into the thriving Centerville.

Meanwhile, Alice Washburn moved into a small, rented apartment with her sister Florence, often dressing like a Victorian dowager in a fine black dress. Her daughters were able to provide them with food and financial assistance, and Alice and Florence dined by candlelight each night, becoming known in town as "the Orchids" for their grace despite poverty. As a wedding gift to her granddaughter, perhaps for old time's sake, the eighty-two-year-old Alice designed a modest Cape Cod house in Cheshire.

When Alice died in 1958, her death certificate and gravestone both read "wife." Though that was certainly one of her activities, the epitaph does not do justice to the scope of her accomplishments. As Isabel Wilder said, this was "a woman who was crazy about building houses and making people happy with their houses." Luckily, history gave Alice a little more credit. In 1990, a four-month celebration was sponsored by the Eli Whitney Museum. Fourteen hundred people took tours of Alice Washburn's many homes, and her name is now synonymous with quality architecture. To own a Washburn is a source of intense pride.

This amazing woman also helped begin the slow move toward equality in Hamden. For the next few decades, Rachel Hartley would keep the flame of the past alive as city historian and as the first female selectman. The town's first policewoman, Bertha Shea, joined the force the same year that the new law enforcement headquarters appeared next to the Miller Library, while Pauline Schwartz, a professor at Southern Connecticut State College, started Hamden's international ambassador program. And though it would be several decades before Lillian Clayman and Barbara DeNicola would reach the highest office of mayor, it was already clear that women had taken the lead building the suburban world of the twentieth century.

CHAPTER 9

Saving the Giant

In 1875, twelve-year-old Arnold Dana and his friends George Woolsey and the Fisher brothers, stopped for sugar cookies and took the train to Mount Carmel. From there they walked to the Sleeping Giant, clambering over its mighty head. The warm day made the boys thirsty, and as they made their way down the Giant's chin they rushed a little. All of a sudden Arnold Dana "slid off into space." He cried out, "I am killed!" and lost consciousness. Dana fell over one hundred feet, smashing into tree limbs and rocks. When he woke, he found that he could not move to escape the flies feeding on him. He waited for what seemed an eternity while his friend Will Fisher clung to the cliff face, trapped on a ledge. Finally, Willis Miller and a group from Mount Carmel arrived with a lumber wagon from the Axle Shop to bring home Dana's dead body. They were happily surprised.

Arnold's body was covered in bruises, both arms were broken and he kept a scar on his left hand until the end of his days. However, this was a small price to pay for a fall that should have killed him outright. Perhaps he was helped by his heredity as the great-grandson of Jonathan Trumbull, champion of the Revolution and governor of Connecticut. Though he thanked his rescuers, and no doubt his strong limbs, Dana always claimed, "The Giant saved me." Perhaps it was because of that belief that little Arnold would one day grow up to help save the mountain for future generations of children.

Though not a particularly tall formation, the Giant had the undeniable shape of a sleeping person, inspiring generations of people to speak of the "left knee" or "right ear" of the mountain. It could also be spotted from leagues away. Centuries before Arnold Dana was born, an innkeeper in the

The idyllic view of Sleeping Giant from the farmland by the Cheshire border was about to be scarred by the excavation of the mountain. *Courtesy of the Hamden Historical Society.*

Catskill Mountains asked a number of New Haven colonists, "What do you call that mountain just north of you, which we see from here on a favorable day?" To them it was the Blue Hills, due to the cerulean haze that seemed to surround it. During the eighteenth century settlers named it Mount Carmel, and during the nineteenth, many began calling it the Dead Indian, perhaps to honor the spirits of those now gone from the land. Supposedly, those Indians named the Giant "Hobbomock," after an evil spirit who, angry at the neglect of his people, stamped a foot and changed the course of the Connecticut River to the east. Before he could do further damage, Kietan, spirit of good, cast a spell on the furious deity so that he lay down and slept, his body strangely perpendicular to the main ridges in Connecticut, with his head at the Mill River and his feet at the Quinnipiac.

Interestingly, geologists would later prove that the legends of the Indians had basis in reality and that the course of the Connecticut River had indeed moved away from the valley where the Quinnipiac flows today. They also had their own ideas about the formation of the mountain. Volcanic eruptions millions of years ago had created the columns of basalt that give it structure, as evidenced by the remnants of an extinct volcano mouth on the fifth ridge. When glaciers swept through in more recent geologic times, they scraped and carved the old trap rock into crags and peaks. Then rivers and streams did their work, creating gorges and valleys, giving the distinctive shape that would later inspire so many legends.

As early as 1721, an effort had been made to preserve this unique range of hills. A common field had been laid out by the New Haven Colony on the slopes, and later Hamden citizens voted to use this British tradition to enclose the hills in a fence. Those who wanted to impound cattle, horses or sheep on the hills had to pay a fee. Prospectors dug a few shafts to mine copper but never found enough to sustain a long-term operation. In 1830, William Haswell lived in a covered wagon on the chest while surveying for the U.S. government. Farmers and tramps used the ancient Quinnipiac Indian trails to cross north to Cheshire and avoid the turnpike. But by 1842, the common field tradition and law had fallen by the wayside, and the fence had been left to ruin.

Then people began building summer houses on the ridges. Willis Cook carted materials up the steep, rocky head to build a house held in place by cables. Houses by David Weiser, the Brocketts and the Matthews sprang up. Frank Elwood Brown designed Cedarhurst on the right arm, while Orrin Dickerman called his cabin, On a Rock. Clarence Conklin built one in the shape of a railroad signal tower. F.A. Park built a house out of the native trap rock with an ivy-covered porch on the edge of the cliff. Nearby, a healer named Miss Demaroy built a tarpaper shack and gathered herbs and brewed salves on the slopes of the hills. It was a fine place for it, since the jumble of hills held microclimates that protected hundreds of plants. Milkweed, chickweed and loosestrife fringed the borders, while star grass and periwinkles, Indian pipe and geraniums could be found along the trails. Children delighted in finding the carnivorous sundew and pitcher plants. Couples walked up from the surrounding villages to pick blueberries every summer. And other edibles like wild carrot, ginger, plantains and parsnips could be found by those with the ancient skills and lore.

On a different kind of search in April 1873, two young boys named Fred Brockett and Homer Tuttle tried to find the mysterious Abraham's Cave and instead found a dead body in fashionable boots. After an investigation, a handkerchief was found with the initials "E.B." It turned out to be Edward Barnum, nephew of the world-famous showman. He had disappeared from his job at the Howe Sewing Machine Company with a bottle of laudanum. P.T. Barnum's nephew's death inspired new interest in the winding fissure now renamed Dead Man's Cave. From his family's cottage, a white one-room building with a porch on the side, Fred Brockett began to take guests and sightseers down into the cave, carrying candles and telling the story to excited ears. However, once a woman got stuck in the narrow lower passageway, Brockett reluctantly stopped his tours.

John H. Dickerman, descendant of the original settler of 1792, built a cottage on the mountain in 1875. On July 4, 1888, he opened a carriage drive to the fourth ridge of what he called Blue Hills Park. "Tables and outfit in pleasant groves on the top, will be offered free on that day to all who will join in a basket picnic." Many joined him at a pavilion, and more summer houses sprung up in the area the road serviced. Dickerman later wrote a book called the *Colonial History of the Parish of Mount Carmel* and a book of poetry called *Legends of the Blue Hills*. The Sleeping Giant's increasing fame, private tours and pleasurable activities began to come together in the minds of Hamden's residents. As geologist and author William P. Blake said in his *History of the Town of Hamden*, "The Blue Hills may become another great public park to give pleasure and health to thousands yet unborne." It was an idea that would have to wait a little longer.

Of course, Hamden already offered plenty of outdoor recreation. Since the Whitney family had enlarged the dam on the Mill River, "Lake Whitney" had become a treasured recreation spot for boating and ice-skating. Residents and tourists alike shopped at Day's Store and walked through the groves of pink mountain laurel. At one time, the Yale crew had used the Mill River, but the members moved their practices and regattas to the lake, and the calls of the coxswain could be heard echoing from the hills. Boathouses lined the shores near the Hartford Turnpike, and Lake Whitney became a spot for citizens to beat the heat for seventy years.

In 1880, the nearby hill of East Rock, shared with New Haven, was bought and protected. This rocky crag that divided the Quinnipiac and Mill Rivers had a strange history before that; it was owned for years by a hermit named Seth Turner and then purchased in 1855 by a man who built a forty-foot boat on the summit of the rock, anticipating a second biblical flood. When it was finally designated a park, Donald Mitchell, a New Haven author, designed carriage drives that led to panoramic views. The magnificent purple-leafed beeches at the spring entrance to East Rock fell within Hamden's boundaries.

The other mountain shared by the two towns was West Rock, though in this case only the south-facing cliffs and the famous Judge's Cave lay within New Haven. A long north–south ridge with a gentle eastern slope hemmed in and protected Hamden, cradling the sparkling waters of Lake Wintergreen. In 1891, the land was acquired for West Rock Park, protecting this natural border from development. Trails led up to an impressive cliff walk, where Hamden residents could look west from their valleys to the world beyond. But the most spectacular cliffs of all were at the Sleeping Giant. Why had they never been protected?

Though initially the quarry company claimed it would not need to dig into the mountain itself, eventually the top of the head was entirely scooped out. *Courtesy of Amy Nawrocki.*

In 1912, this oversight would come back to haunt the town. The Mount Carmel Traprock Company obtained a lease to quarry the head, and soon the peace of the village was disturbed daily by blasting dynamite. Carts piled with eight tons of gravel wobbled out along a new causeway across the Mill River, which was soon choked with dust. Roads all over America needed gravel to handle the new motorcars, and the bones of the Giant worked well. However, the townsfolk immediately protested, skeptical of the company's assertion that it was "not going east into the rock…His head is too hard and too large to be disturbed by such picayune operations as are going on here." A smaller hill in southern Hamden—Pine Rock—had already been mined since 1910, leaving nothing but a blasted shell. The years would prove the protestors' suspicions correct.

Decades after his encounter with a dead man at Abraham's Cave, Fred Brockett still enjoyed his cabin on the Giant with its thirty-foot platform tower. In a fateful decision, he invited William Avis, an outdoor enthusiast who swam in Long Island Sound every day and worked as a correspondent for the *New Haven Register*. Now a venerable judge, Brockett showed Avis the glacial erratics and hidden ponds, the splashing waterfalls and hanging valleys. Avis described sunset at the cabin: "Over all this beautiful and enchanting panorama fell the warm rays of the first westering sun and as we swept the circle once more no man spoke." A man named James Toumey from the Yale School of Forestry happened to read this article and decided to try to create a park.

World War I temporarily interfered with his plans, but in March 1924, Toumey formed the Sleeping Giant Park Association (SGPA) to buy as much as it could "for use as a park, forest, or game preserve…with the eventual purpose of transferring the same for the use and benefit of the public." Toumey promoted common ownership, an idea that echoed the growing national park movement of the time. However, this was not an idle project. Every day, open quarrying emptied out more and more of the top of the Giant's head to crush for paving rock. Eli Whitney Blake had invented the stone crusher so many decades earlier, and now it was the association's duty to stop it.

One hundred people joined at the first meeting. Arnold Dana had spent thirty-five years in New York working for the editorial staff of the *Commercial and Financial Chronicle*. Now back in Connecticut, he dedicated himself to the preservation of the Giant. William Avis, still writing furiously, donated land as well as his pen. "Up! Up! Remember Paul Revere! George Washington at Valley Forge! No task to us should seem severe, to save our Giant from the Scourge!" he wrote. A descendant of Hamden's most famous family, Susan Whitney was also an early leader. They would form the core of a dedicated group that would transform the landscape of Hamden, not by developing it, but by preserving it.

The fight brought in warriors from every segment of society. Amos Wilder, father of famous author Thornton, wrote an editorial in 1928, saying, "All New Haven County may be said to have a stake in the beautiful enterprise." He and his wife, Isabella, also pledged money to the cause. Alice Tyler wrote a letter in support but was too old, deaf and poor to help. Her husband had recently died as he was in the process of telling her that beauty and truth were comingled. "When I see New Haven and Hamden allowing the Sleeping Giant to disappear, I feel as if everybody were deaf to that truth which my husband knew, that was the secret of my husband's life," she said. "But we who are left can push toward it, and you certainly are doing your bit in saving the Sleeping Giant."

The LaFarge family joined the cause as well. They had moved to Reverend Joseph Brewster's house on Spruce Bank Road along the Mill River in 1915. Bancel LaFarge's father had been a celebrated artist in the late nineteenth century, and his son was following his lead creating beautiful altarpieces, church windows and murals. He also dabbled in architecture, restoring one of James Ives's houses. Bancel had married Mabel Hooper, the niece of his father's friend Henry Adams, historian and American royalty. Mabel was a watercolorist and still life painter and had a "faculty for getting at the genius of a flower." One of her paintings had even adorned her uncle's famous autobiography, *The Education of Henry Adams*. Though they were friends with the rich and famous around the world, this talented family directed their wealth and creativity to serve their community.

The association had an early success when the 1792 house belonging to Jonathan Dickerman II, uncle of Ezra and the three sisters, was donated to the SGPA. However, a setback occurred when the local trap rock company sold out to a big corporation, Blakeslee Associates, which had no connection to Hamden. The rock fell faster and more indiscriminately, and the booming cracks of dynamite echoed down the valley. The association also chipped away desperately, continuing to increase the acreage of the planned park. Mount Carmel schoolchildren donated pennies to buy land from reluctant owners. By 1930, they had 845 acres, but the head eluded them. Finally, a campaign was started, and enough money was raised in ninety days to buy the last piece of the Giant. In 1930, Dana said to the group, "Hail to the happy day which unites us in a crusade so worthy of our lineage—a crusade to preserve this unique and priceless legacy, a mountain beloved from time immemorial as an inspiration and joy." He also asked, "What is a Sleeping Giant without a head?" and said, "We may be a little body, but we are far more representative of the community surrounding the mountain than many imagine." However, the corporation refused the deal, asking for even more money. The quarrying continued and the rock crusher rolled on, the lease unbroken and seemingly unassailable.

The Sleeping Giant Park Association celebrates its victory buying the last piece of the mountain in 1933. *Courtesy of the Hamden Historical Society.*

The SGPA turned to the law and found that the damage to the head reached up to a point where it violated the lease since it could be seen from the road. Would it prevail on a technicality? Almost, but not quite. The lease needed to be bought out, and the money that the corporation asked for was outrageous and its conditions too extreme. James Toumey had died and Dana was discouraged, so Helen Porter, one of the directors, took charge of the situation in July 1933. Porter was on the boards of all of the local charity organizations and believed in her civic duties. She shook thousands of hands to convince citizens and landowners—thankless, tedious work. With all of the negative publicity, the quarrymen became pariahs in town, and when the manager was ordered to quarry along the north face, he balked. Even the wives of the workers began to make things unpleasant for their husbands. Still, Blakeslee Associates refused to leave. Porter sent telegrams, wrote letters and made countless phone calls. She raised $32,000 in the middle of the Great Depression to pay the lease. She then faced the head of Blakeslee and talked him down from three more years of quarrying to zero. When honored by the town, she said, "I feel like a French girl praised for saving her mother from a burning house. It just had to be done." The Sleeping Giant was left with a terrible head wound but would recover.

This success inspired more preservation around Hamden. In 1932, Franklin Roosevelt's Work Projects Administration started work on Baldwin Drive in West Rock Park, paralleling the Regicides Trail. A bequest of Governor Simeon Baldwin, the drive provided a long ridge road four hundred feet above the surrounding lands, with fine views to both the west and east. Soon, couples rode bicycles along the flat, curving crest or drove up for romantic necking at a sunset lookout. Eventually, West Rock's Lake Wintergreen was taken out of the water supply and become a haven for boating and fishing. On the other side of town people walked from the old Whitney factories over a replica of the Ithiel Town truss bridge, heading past the old smithy into the forests of East Rock. The beech trees in the Hamden section grew enormous, their purplish leaves shining beacons beckoning children to climb into their huge branches. At the north end, Brooksvale Park was officially created in 1947. The one-hundred-acre Brooks Farm had been a place to house the town's poor since about 1856 but had fallen into disuse. At first it was just a typical town park, but in 1960 it was rededicated to nature recreation and education. With its small zoo of rabbits, goats and peacocks, Brooksvale became a hit with the children of the town, and activities such as camping and maple sugaring followed. Jim Grandy was hired by the town as a ranger and moved in to become an enthusiastic caretaker for thirty-five years.

Tales from the Sleeping Giant

After years of protest, the freight train was relocated to the east along the border with North Haven to avoid the nuisance of noise and danger so close to the main thoroughfare. Neighborhoods began to carefully preserve their own parks and green spaces. The Spring Glen Civic Association worked to save a glacial kettle sink near Lake Whitney called Johnson's Pond. This tiny ecosystem cradled yellow-crowned night herons and chickadees, nuthatches and red-bellied woodpeckers. The wild cherry, Canada mayflower and maple leaf viburnum would be allowed to grow unhindered by suburban progress. It seemed that everyone was trying to live up to W.H. Avis's pronouncement in the *New Haven Register*:

> *Blessed by nature in almost every conceivable way, with beautiful scenery, fertile soil, pleasant valleys, rugged hills, gem-like lakes, musical brooks, emerald woods, sweet pure air, and mellow sunshine, the town of Hamden is indeed one of the jewel spots of all the earth.*

Meanwhile, a near-deaf Arnold Dana resigned from his post as SGPA president in 1935. The association's work seemed done, with responsibility for the Sleeping Giant now with the State Park Commission. But the members decided against disbanding, vowing to continue their duty as active citizens. Bancel LaFarge took up the presidency and set about planning the path system. J. Walter Bassett, a veteran of World War I, formed a nature trail committee and, with an army of volunteers, spun out the first web of blazes. Roosevelt's WPA crew built a 10 percent graded path up the Giant, and LaFarge designed a Norman-style tower using stones from the old Park family house, the last remaining on the chest. The head of the WPA project happened to be Harry Webb, a friend of Bancel, and both worked on this project until the artist died. Bassett took over as president and led Mabel LaFarge and other members up the new switchback path, winding through mountain laurel, around the second ridge and onto the highest point, where they climbed the ramp of the four-story stone tower.

This simple walk would become one of the most popular trails in the entire state, increasing the park's visitors from fifty-six hundred to seventy thousand in just two years. And every year more and more came, and more fell in love. Still, Helen Porter and the remaining members kept vigilant. In 1947, Dana died, and Porter bolted a bronze tablet to a rock on the Tower Trail dedicated to his strange journey from near-death fall to liberator. Of course, Arnold Dana was not alone in his achievement. Helen Porter, William Avis, James Toumey, Fred Brockett, Bancel LaFarge and thousands

Artist Bancel LaFarge designed this Norman castle tower for the highest point on the Sleeping Giant, using stones from the old Park family house. *Courtesy of the author.*

of others accomplished what no single person could have done—saving land that would become the most celebrated park in the state.

In 1948, children's author Eleanor Estes published a collection of fiction called *Sleeping Giant and Other Stories*, in which the mountain arises from its slumber and walks. It has been a common fantasy, shared by storytellers from the Quinnipiac Indians to U.S. poet laureate Donald Hall. But in reality, it was the people who loved the Giant who awoke. Now, future generations can walk his safe and sleeping limbs to hear the click of a woodpecker's beak or smell wild sarsaparilla. They can spot owls in hollow oaks and trace the stonework of colonial farmers. And in his story they may find truth: that as long as people band together to save the things they love, there may be hope, not just for wild places, but also for the humans who walk amongst them.

CHAPTER 10

Toying with Paradise

Alfred Carlton Gilbert always hated his first name, preferring the initials "A.C." However, he took a lot of pride in his last name, and though he was born in Salem, Oregon, he always boasted that his family had been in the New Haven Colony from the beginning. "It's strange to think that when I came from three thousand miles across the country from where I was born and settled down, I chose, without realizing it, a spot near the original homes of my ancestors." It's likely that he was distantly related to Captain John Gilbert, that early martyr of the Revolution, and descended from Matthew Gilbert, co-founder of the New Haven Colony. Those connections through the centuries are no doubt one reason why A.C. Gilbert dreamed of building paradise in Hamden's green hills.

Growing up in the 1890s, Gilbert was a short, thin child with jug-handle ears and big brown eyes, often picked on at school. This only made him more determined to pursue dreams of athletic glory, and he set about turning himself into solid muscle. Though he grew to a modest five feet, seven inches and 135 pounds, he became a national champion in college wrestling, won awards at sprints and hurdles, quarterbacked the Yale football team and, in 1906, at New York's Celtic Park, pole vaulted twelve feet, three inches, the world record at the time. Somehow he found time to get a medical degree from Yale University, but instead of going into practice, he decided to become a magician.

In 1911, he and his new wife, Mary, and their daughter lived in an apartment in New Haven. He made a small living performing at $100 shows all over Connecticut and New York, following in the tracks of Harry Houdini.

A.C. Gilbert confronted the challenges of life head-on and triumphed. *Courtesy of the Hamden Historical Society.*

Along the way, he invented many do-it-yourself tricks and marketed them, finding partners to help with financing. When performing in New York City, he sold his magic tricks to interested shops and suppliers. One night, after seeing the new construction along the rail line, he was intrigued by the new steel beams. The next day, he and his wife cut pieces out of cardboard, and he took them to a machine shop, which turned the small models into steel. After tinkering with the design, he finally figured out what he called the "perfect girder." Mary Gilbert nursed their child and watched her husband play with his new bars and brackets with amusement, hardly thinking that this new project might lead to international fame and fortune. Gilbert's partners in the magic business were less amused and didn't want anything to do with this strange new game. His father, disappointed with his son's choice of career, nevertheless floated him a loan to develop this toy. Of course, as A.C. Gilbert was the first to point out, the Erector Set could hardly be called a toy. It was science.

Gilbert rented an old carriage factory near Yale for eighteen months and developed the first Erector Set, adding a small motor to improve the kit. By 1913, he was ready for the New York Toy Fair, where he wowed toy stores, receiving more orders than he could fill. From a new factory by the railroad tracks, he began producing thousands upon thousands of these sets, now nicknamed "the world's greatest toy." He quickly expanded, producing America's first "real" children's weather kits, astronomy kits and chemistry sets. He used contests and monthly magazines to popularize these unusual products, binding his new fans into a nationwide community. In 1915, sixty thousand letters with photos of new Erector Set designs flooded the mailbox at the A.C. Gilbert Company, all vying for the grand prize of an actual, adult-sized car. A boy from St. Louis won it with his working model of the Panama Canal.

However, Americans' thoughts were soon turned away from games. The sinking of American ships by German submarines prompted the United States' entry into World War I, and the men of Hamden volunteered to serve. Tim Conroy worked at the Winchester Repeating Arms but joined the navy to fight in the English Channel. Thomas Cote fought at Verdun with neighbor James Denice, who was wounded in the leg and gassed. Dozens of Hamden men fought in the trenches of every battle in France, men like Raymond Alling, Leslie Bottomley, Harold and Stanley Leeke, Harry Nelson and John Sanford. Many were wounded, and some, like Russell Mansfield, earned distinction in the field of battle. Amos Niven Wilder, brother of the famous writer, received a Croix de Guerre as an ambulance driver. Most, like Bernard Fitch or George Kreis, entered service as privates, fought in the fields and forests of France and returned to resume their quiet jobs as electricians or typewriter mechanics. But not everyone made it back. John McDermott was the first Hamden soldier to die on April 15, 1918, at Seicheprey. Maurice Collins was killed in the Argonne, and others followed as America struggled through the bloody and destructive war.

Meanwhile, in September 1918, A.C. Gilbert was called to the War Department, which was ready to turn America's toy manufacturers into munitions plants and ban toy sales that Christmas. After all, toys were not part of the war effort, and everyone was making sacrifices. However, Gilbert made his own argument adroitly. "America is the home of toys that educate as well as amuse, that visualize to the boy his future occupations." Without them, he said, "the country will lose a generation of doctors, engineers, and scientists." Then, like a master magician, he pulled out a selection of toys and set them on the table in front of the group of serious and politically jaded men. Within minutes, they were playing with them. The Council on National Defense did not ban toy sales that Christmas. The *Boston Post* declared, "Cabinet Members Become Boys Again." The caption by their photo of A.C. Gilbert read, "The Man Who Saved Christmas for the

Children." But Gilbert demurred at this, and the reporter quoted him as saying, "I didn't do it. Tell them it was their own toys that won the day."

Gilbert's factory did in fact help during the war, however. It fashioned parts for machine guns and gas masks, as well as Colt .45 automatics on subcontract from Winchester. When the war ended, it returned to what it did best, and by 1926, college chemistry classes filled up with boys raised on Gilbert's chemistry sets. But Gilbert himself was already onto his next idea: radio. In the rear of his factory, he built radio station WCJ, the fifth licensed station in the country. In 1928, he sponsored the first national sports broadcasts review program, with himself as the eager host. And, of course, he sold beginner radio sets to legions of children, helping to start a national pastime.

Until now, Gilbert had little connection with Hamden, other than as an admirer and employer of many workers from this northern suburb. However, with the money he made from his booming toy business, he bought a huge chunk of land on both sides of Ridge Road. Using rough-cut fieldstones, Gilbert built a fifteen-room, Tudor-style mansion with lead-paned windows set deep in wide stone walls. His wife named it Maraldene. Soon, it included a nine-hole golf course in the backyard, an Olympic-sized swimming pool, formal garden, kennels to breed German shepherds and a mossy, man-made waterfall. Inside, visitors found antique English furniture, a movie projection room and a trophy case with 150 awards from pole vault, wrestling, horizontal bar, rope climbing and golf. A lover of Connecticut's state flower, Gilbert found a wonderful stand of two-hundred-year-old mountain laurel in western Hamden and planted it around his yard.

Gilbert was not resting on those laurels, however. "Standing still is all that bothers me," he often said. He loved sweets and desserts, but his constant regimen of exercise kept him without a potbelly his whole life. The Maraldene gymnasium included a rowing machine, Indian clubs, dumbbells and a punching bag. He installed a chin-up bar at the factory. An avid hunter, he took trips to British Columbia and the Gaspe Peninsula, racking up eighteen North American big game records. He shot and edited nature films on these journeys, showing them at lunch hour in the factory and at lectures throughout America. He also pursued his interest in hunting and fishing in Hamden itself, buying the six-hundred-acre tract of land on Dunbar Hill where he found his mountain laurel, calling it the Gilbert Game Preserve.

This preserve would become his true delight. Home to thousands of ducks, woodchucks and foxes, Gilbert found what might have been the last real wilderness in the city limits. The area had been called Little Egypt by locals and had been a Quinnipiac hunting ground. After buying the land in

1930, he built a cabin there a year later, blazing his own trails in this recently reforested area and hunting for deer and quail. He dug a trout pond on the hill close enough to fish from his porch. During the 1930s, he planted seven hundred apple trees and added seven ponds, twenty bridges and a herd of Jersey cattle. Eventually, he raised chickens and turkeys, and the small dairy supplied the cafeteria at his New Haven factory. He made use of everything, and even the flies killed on the farm went into the microscope sets. At the cabin, he hosted generals and admirals every year after the Army/Navy game played at the Yale Bowl. Then, in 1937, W.O. Cohen came to the lodge to hunt deer but ended up selling his model train company, American Flyer. Gilbert added his own improvements—like engines that smoked and whistled—created the first actual "two-rail" track and endeavored to make accurate reproductions of the cars, using the actual blueprints from railroad companies. Because of, or perhaps despite, this continued success, he seemed to spend less time in his walnut-paneled office and more in his new "Paradise."

While Gilbert found sanctuary in the hills of Hamden, others saw it as the perfect place for business. In 1915, the American Mills Company took over the Web Company, which had in turn taken over the old Candee Factory in Centerville. The Marlin Rockwell Corporation built a munitions factory in Highwood during World War I. The Acme Wire Company built a factory on Dixwell Avenue, and the Detroit Steel Corporation opened on State Street. The Mayo Radiator Company fabricated radiators for newfangled automobiles, while the Whitney-Blake Manufacturing Company began to make electric fittings in Hamden.

A mason from Italy named Ciro Paolella clearly saw the opportunity in Hamden to turn his dreams into reality. He moved to town in 1913 and married a woman named Mary Jane. A few years later, he expanded his small home business making concrete blocks, moving to a corner of Dixwell Avenue and calling it the Hamden Building Tile Company. After eking through the Depression, he changed its name to the Plasticrete Corporation in 1945. Paolella employed dozens of people, bought the Hamden-based Connecticut Brick Company and the Stiles Company and supplied many of the town's building projects with materials. His sales reached the millions in the 1950s and kept going up. In fact, this family-run business continued to grow until it produced 100,000 concrete blocks a day, a testament to Ciro's American dream.

A.C. Gilbert's own dreams seemed to multiply as he aged. His Hall of Science in Manhattan dazzled young boys and girls with American Flyers,

The workers of the Web Shop in Centerville helped build Hamden's industry, and during World War I it would assist in the war effort. *Courtesy of the Hamden Historical Society.*

Erector Sets and models that came to life. He also sat on the American Olympic Committee and the executive board of the Track and Field Committee. Due to his argument, the United States switched to the metric system in track and field so that American athletes could be considered for all international records. It was not just serious work that inspired him. Often he would perform magic tricks for friends and neighborhood children. The Christmas after Charles Lindbergh's transatlantic flight, the residents of Hamden were shocked to see a low-flying plane dipping over the golf courses and parks. A parachutist landed on Gilbert's lawn, and everyone was astonished to find that it was Santa Claus.

Gilbert continued to keep himself fit by waking up at 6:00 a.m. and running a morning mile in Spring Glen, then working his punching bag in the basement gym before heading to the factory, often in a hunting outfit or track suit. He devoted countless hours to the art of the pole vault, studying hundreds of hours of film of the world's best pole-vaulters. He often worked with other Olympic pole-vaulters in the backyard of Maraldene and was considered by many to be the world's leading authority. Finishing the work that the Webbs and Alice Washburn began in Spring Glen, he built residential neighborhoods on the ever-shifting border between Hamden and North Haven. Making sure that "each road had a parkway down the middle," he rebuilt old farmhouses into modern ones and unselfishly chopped up the Maraldene property to help the community of Spring Glen develop fully.

The sesquicentennial in 1936 provided much-needed relief from the Great Depression as the entire town joined together in celebration. *Courtesy of the Hamden Historical Society.*

The great-grandson of the original owner of Spring Glen, Edward Gosselin, happened to be stationed at Pearl Harbor in 1941. On December 7, Ensign Gosselin was on the battleship USS *Arizona* and was killed in the Japanese attack. Another Hamden man, Harry Torgerson, was on an LST (tank landing) ship that had been destroyed nearby but swam to shore and survived. This tragic attack transformed the town, putting all of its citizens on alert. Some Hamden natives, like Ernest Borgnine, were already members of the armed forces. Borgnine's immigrant parents met and married in Hamden and lived there during the Depression on Cherry Ann Street. "My favorite activity was hiking on Pine Rock Mountain," he once said, though he also enjoyed stealing apples from the Farnhams' orchard. His navy service had ended in 1941, but Borgnine reenlisted immediately when the United States entered World War II, serving until 1945 and reaching the rank of gunner's mate first class. Of course, he would go on to have a long film and television career, supporting the navy his entire life.

Others from Hamden soon joined the war effort. Francis O' Connor, editor of the *Hamden Chronicle*, later recalled:

> *One morning in June of our senior year the radios crackled with the news of the Allied invasion of Italy. For my contemporaries it meant two things: the big push to end the war was on, and the need for massive troop replacements was upon us. Our time was falling due. Many graduated early and enlisted in the service, months before the scheduled end of their high school days. Some were propelled into the thick of the Battle of the Bulge and the push*

into Germany. A boyhood friend had enlisted in the marines and within a
year was dead in the ashes of a place called Iwo Jima in the south Pacific.

Marcus McCraven, who later became vice-president of the United Illuminating Company and president of the Quinnipiac Club, served as an expert rifleman. Arthur Burns enlisted in the navy and took part in the D-day invasion. Alex Civitello marched through France, avoiding mines and sharpshooters. John Endiss, later a Hamden police officer, joined the navy in 1943. He helped liberate the Marshall Islands, fighting through the terrible stench of dead bodies, and later survived an attack by a kamikaze pilot near Okinawa. Merchant marine Marshall Dunbar's ship was sunk in the icy North Sea, but he was pulled out of the water by a Dutch ship. The Dutchmen served him a hot cup of "Netherlands coffee," which included fish heads. He drank it anyway, glad to have survived.

Men were not the only ones who sacrificed for the war effort. Ruth Cook was a college student during World War II and drove an eighteen-wheeler loaded with ammunition all over the United States. "I never told my parents," she said. Shirley Sutherland joined WAVES, the women's branch of the U.S. Navy, later marching ahead of the coffin of President Roosevelt from Union Station to the White House. And hundreds of Hamden women worked tirelessly in factories and in living rooms to make sure that the "boys over there" succeeded. Gas rationing in Hamden prevented them from driving far to church, leading to the formation of such community churches as Dunbar United. Their children hid under the desks during air raid drills. These citizens—along with soldiers like Walter Parmelee, wounded at Saipan; and Kenneth Harrington, barely alive in a German POW camp—sacrificed much for their own American dreams.

During the war, A.C. Gilbert won approval from Congress to continue making his Erector Sets and educational toys, but the factory did switch to war work eventually, producing parts for parachutes, mines, flares and machine guns. The factory even developed the use of enamel coating for motor wires. It would help indirectly as well when the American model of the portable bridge used for crossing rivers in World War II was built with an Erector Set. When the war finally ended, Gilbert quickly switched back to civilian products. The little toy tank became a Caterpillar tractor, and the model airplane craze started with his rubber band Air-Kraft toy. However, the sacrifices of employees like Albert Redway, who had served in the war, inspired Gilbert to give something back. After World War II, he began converting part of his paradise estate into a private country club for

This aerial shot of the center of Hamden also shows the hills to the west, where A.C. Gilbert hunted, fished and later built his Paradise. *Courtesy of the Hamden Historical Society.*

his employees and their families. Though he was over sixty years old, Gilbert was in fantastic shape and did much of the brush clearing and building himself. The club opened in 1947 with a picnic attended by fifteen hundred people competing on the softball fields, rowing on its two small lakes, eating refreshments in its pavilion and barbecuing in the stone fireplaces. Though this country club was soon annexed by the community, as Gilbert said, "Thousands of people have gained great pleasure from it."

Gilbert also helped improve Paradise Avenue, paved Dunbar Hill Road and began planning new roads in this remote area of town. Carving up his Paradise estate to share with others, he developed Laurel Hills, with small houses for his workers. Soon, the Gilberts joined them, selling Maraldene and building their new house, Mountain View, around the old hunting lodge on Dunbar Hill. Though much of the six hundred acres was now residential neighborhood, deer still browsed through the oaks and dogwoods. "Life can never be dull when there are animals around," A.C. often said. A huge picture window looked out on the forested hills of Hamden and down into the spires of New Haven. Now closing in on seventy years old, he often sat on this terrace and threw his fishing line into the trout pond, enjoying the fruits of his dreams. Athlete, magician, inventor, entrepreneur and genius, A.C. Gilbert was just one of many who found paradise in the hills of Hamden, Connecticut.

CHAPTER II

Our Town

When the nomadic Wilder family moved to Hamden in 1915, daughter Isabel probably had no intention of settling down. She had attended thirteen high schools and escaped the earthquake in San Francisco by only ten days. To her, it seemed to be just another stop on a whirlwind tour of the world. Soon afterward, her brother Thornton transferred to nearby Yale, after discovering the wonders of the library in Dwight Hall, designed so many years earlier by Henry Austin. Isabel asked her brother, "Do you think you'll ever have a book in this library?" He told her, "I've thought about it, Isabel; but I'd have to be about fifty before I could hope to write a book that would be good enough for Yale." It would not take quite that long.

With money tight, Thornton and Isabel's parents rented a crumbling Cape Cod house in Mount Carmel. Their father, Amos Parker Wilder, had attended Yale, taught, written for newspapers, edited a journal and become the consul general in Hong Kong. Poor health had forced him out of the consular service, and he returned to Yale with his family to teach and write. He taught his sons and daughters that achieving character was the highest goal a person could have.

Their mother, Isabella, was a voluminous reader, avid translator and amateur poet. She encouraged her family to live at the center of the cultural community and to discover truth for themselves. She introduced her children to the classics, took them to the theatre and encouraged them to study music and culture. Thornton once called her "one of Shakespeare's girls—a star danced and under it I was born." Isabella was elected to the school board in 1918, the first elected female in Hamden history, one year before women could even vote. The men on the board smoked their cigars and watched her suspiciously. She ignored them and helped bring Hamden education into the twentieth century. She was "the most intelligent woman I had ever known," Thornton always declared.

These two parents would produce children who succeeded beyond their wildest aspirations. Eldest son Amos Niven wrote essays and poetry at Yale, where he received his PhD, and somehow found time to become a ranked tennis champion. During World War I, he entered the American Field Service and became an artillery corporal in the Expeditionary Forces. Charlotte and Janet attended Mount Holyoke College and were excellent students. Isabel entered the first class of the Yale School of Drama. And then there was Thornton. Despite poor eyesight, he tried to serve in World War I and was able to enlist in the Coast Artillery, later acting as assistant secretary to the Clearance Committee War Industries Board. Stationed at Fort Adams in Newport, Rhode Island, he was eventually promoted to corporal. Returning to Hamden, he began to write feverishly, serving on Yale's *Literary Magazine* and finishing his degree. Throughout the early 1920s, he rambled around the world, attending different colleges and teaching at different schools. He seemed less driven than his siblings, except maybe Isabel, with whom he shared a special bond.

Then, his first novel, *The Cabala*, was published in 1926. It was not a huge success, but the next year Thornton struck gold with *The Bridge of San Luis Rey*. This seemingly simple story asked the question of why bad things happen to good people by exploring the stories of those who die in a random bridge collapse in Peru. It won the Pulitzer Prize and spawned a century of disaster fiction that followed Wilder's model. More importantly for the struggling Wilder family, it brought Thornton huge critical and commercial success. He was in demand everywhere.

In 1929, he lost his voice after a lecture series and returned home, where his delighted family hovered over him. This may have been when Thornton's plans for them came into focus. He ordered a house built by local architect Alice Washburn on the slopes of Mill Rock, above the old Whitney factory. His parents, Isabel and Janet moved into this rambling wooden structure, calling it fondly, "the house that *The Bridge* built." Their road, Deepwood Drive, was becoming a famous address where people such as William P. Blake (in the 1870s) and J.F. Fulton, famous physiologist and neuroscientist, lived. Thornton called the sharp, red crag of East Rock out his window "our Dolomite" and often said, "I live on a heap of dirt pushed down by an icecap from the north."

Thornton Wilder approached life with a lightness matched only by his gravity as a writer. *Courtesy of the Hamden Historical Society.*

Standing at an acute angle to the road, this brown, shingled house contained a huge living room filled with bookshelves that took up half the first floor. The numerous bedrooms on the second floor included a large master chamber that peered over the small, winding road. Wilder used that for his study. They had a garden, a terrace and, most importantly, privacy. The family could sit at a spacious dinner table while Thornton read works in progress and letters he received from around the world out loud. At last, the migrant Wilders had a place that seemed like home.

While the Wilder family was settling into their new Hamden home thanks to Thornton's success, a future literary icon named Donald Hall was born nearby. Unlike the Wilders, the Halls had been in Hamden for generations. Donald's great-grandfather Charlie had helped build the Whitney reservoir in 1860, living in a small house by the icehouses on the lake. One day, he walked down Whitney Avenue to New Haven and enlisted in the Union army. After the war, Charlie worked on a farm for the Webb family in what would become Spring Glen. Following an argument, he started his own dairy to compete with his former boss, out of spite. Later, he led Charlie Hall's Fife and Drum Corps, playing at local picnics and town functions.

When Donald's grandfather Henry and grandmother Augusta took over the dairy business, she kept the books and he milked the cows. They were still delivering milk by horse and wagon even when Donald was born in 1928. His father, Donald Andrew, had been a member of the Whitneyville Volunteer Fire Department in his teens but then had left Hamden to teach history and English. A budding actress named Bette Davis had received an *A* in his English class. He returned to Hamden with his wife, Lucy, who became president of the Whitneyville Women's Club. They had probably not wanted to own a dairy, but it was doing so well that they couldn't turn it down. Despite the Depression, they built a new brick building on Whitney Avenue in 1934, and a proud young Donald toured his family's new plant with his kindergarten class. Passing cars could see the gleaming bottle-washing machine in the windows, and residents could buy the plant's ice cream, butter and cottage cheese in any of Hamden's general stores. Brock-Hall's "Grade A" cream was soon considered the best in the county.

After a series of rented houses throughout Whitneyville and Spring Glen, the Hall family bought a six-room house with a coal furnace on the corner of Ardmore and Greenway, near Johnson's Pond. Donald walked to the Spring Glen School and sledded on the hill of the old James J. Webb farm. He enjoyed rides around Hamden in the family's brand-new Studebaker and listening to the radio under the covers when he was supposed to be sleeping. Then, at age fourteen, he made a decision that would change his life; he decided to become a poet: "Coming home from high school, I shut the door of my bedroom and sat at my desk, working at poems every afternoon for two hours."

As one might imagine, Donald was often picked on by other boys in his class. "Go and write a poem about it!" they taunted him. So he did. At sixteen, he attended the famed Bread Loaf Writers' Conference and met Robert Frost. That year, he published his first work with Yale University Press, a patriotic lecture about World War II, and began to submit his poetry to magazines. For the Hamden High School literary magazine *The Cupola*, he wrote a poem well beyond his years called "Wind-in-Storm." While still a teenager, he began to report for the New Haven newspapers. He also delved briefly into theatre, playing the drunken choirmaster in Thornton Wilder's new play *Our Town*. Before leaving Hamden for boarding school, he dated the actress playing the tragic Emily, who probably never suspected that her boyfriend would become one of the great poets of the twentieth century.

Our Town was another huge success for Wilder and won him his second Pulitzer Prize. The play followed the ordinary lives of residents in Grover's Corners, New Hampshire, a town that could just as easily have been in Connecticut. Certainly, some of the New England flavor of this bittersweet story came from the author's experiences in Hamden, though its universal values of life and love reached out to the entire world. While championing what some would call traditional values, Wilder had experimented with a

Thornton Wilder's study in his house at Deepwood Drive was his refuge, where he wrote some of his greatest works. *Courtesy of the Hamden Historical Society.*

deconstructive style, a minimalist set and a choric stage manager, pushing the boundaries of the form. He actually played the stage manager on Broadway, cleverly inserting himself into his own work of drama. But he did not rest from constant experimentation. After this success as the only person to ever win the Pulitzer in fiction and drama, he polished up his next play, *The Skin of Our Teeth*, in Hamden to win his third. It was first performed at the Shubert Theatre in New Haven and again spoke of the human condition in a fascinating way, becoming an allegory for the history of civilization.

While Thornton stayed at Deepwood Drive, Isabella and Isabel gathered him into the town's social scene, where he was quickly identified by his ubiquitous brown suits and tortoise-shell glasses. He said of himself, somewhat ironically, "What a fortunate young man, and how devoted to his mother and sister." But he was not always a reliable host. A thought would strike him, and he would sprint up the stairs to write in his journal or make notes for the next project. He made longer escapes, too, taking the train to New York to dine at Twenty-One and spend lots of money. He went farther and farther, headed to Paris or Arizona. But he would always be home for Christmas, when Isabel regaled him with simple soups, kippers and German sausages. The plays *Bernice* and *Wreck of the 5:25* demonstrated the tension Wilder felt between the need for refuge and for travel. That tension would characterize the rest of his life.

During World War II, he left Hamden again to fight for his country. As a celebrity warrior, he met the press at the side of Captain Clark Gable and Don Ameche. He rose to the rank of lieutenant colonel in the army air force and received awards for his diligence. In 1955, Wilder reworked his failed play *The Merchant of Yonkers* into *The Matchmaker*, and it became a smash hit, eventually adapted into the hit musical *Hello, Dolly!* He wrote libretti to two operas and a screenplay to Alfred Hitchcock's *Shadow of a Doubt*. His novel *The Eighth Day* won the National Book Award. Meanwhile, Amos and Isabella died, leaving only Thornton and Isabel at the house. Isabel had cared for her aging parents, and when they were gone, she cared for Thornton, making sure the house was ready for his return.

Throughout these years acting as Thornton's anchor, Isabel pursued a vigorous life of her own. She became the curator of Yale's theatre archive and even wrote three popular novels of her own: *Mother and Four*, *Heart Be Still* and *Let Winter Go*. Thornton's other siblings had left the family in Hamden and gone out into the world. Amos Niven had been ordained a Congregational minister and had become a celebrated professor of theology at Harvard Divinity School. Janet earned a PhD in zoology and taught at Mount Holyoke, writing a memoir about horse rearing and advocating fiercely for animal rights and conservation. Charlotte had won the Shelley Memorial Award for Poetry in 1937 and seemed to be the next Wilder to achieve literary fame. However, she suffered a nervous breakdown and was institutionalized. Thornton and Isabel took financial responsibility for her, and even cared for her for a brief period in the 1950s at Deepwood Drive.

A typical day involved Thornton driving into town for breakfast at 7:00 a.m., reading the newspaper, stopping at the Yale Library and then returning to the study to write. He never owned a television and accomplished a lot in that long, low room overlooking the forest. While listening to Mozart quintets on his turntable, he copied his work from one loose-leaf notebook to another, improving it. He spent long days making notations in his favorite novel, James Joyce's *Finnegan's Wake*. He wrote letters to people like Orson Welles and Gertrude Stein and received them from Robert Frost, Albert Einstein, and thousands of ordinary Americans. Then, the outside world would reach in and snatch Thornton away. Montgomery Clift stopped by to begin their friendship. Invitations arrived for him to teach at universities across the country. In 1962, he drove from Hamden to Washington, D.C.,

An elderly Isabel Wilder laughs while attending the dedication of the Thornton Wilder Hall at Hamden's Miller Library. *Courtesy of the Hamden Historical Society.*

for an evening entertaining the Kennedy cabinet, reading from his works. He won the Presidential Medal of Freedom the next year.

Isabel saw her primary job as the guardian of Thornton's fame and prosperity from their home in Hamden, turning away countless fans and curiosity seekers. She clipped newspaper articles about his plays and novels, keeping careful track of his successes. She also defended his right to a confidential personal life, squashing speculation about his sexuality. This strange alliance would have destroyed many siblings, but their affection held strong. Besides, she enjoyed her access to celebrities and scholars, financial security and opportunity to travel around the world. Occasionally, she and Thornton would take his Thunderbird to New York to watch plays, and they often dined at fine restaurants around Connecticut. Her brother left and returned to Hamden time and time again, caught between his love of travel and the need for peace and privacy.

For Wilder, Hamden was a place of quiet and solitude to return to after seeking knowledge in the wider world. But for others, Hamden seemed like the perfect place to expand learning. After World War II, Edward and Adele Paier began a small art school, moving to Hamden in 1956. The husband-and-wife team started as the only full-time teachers, instructing students in their house how to make commercial art and design. Edward painted portraits to make ends meet. Adele had a head for business and helped the school through its difficult early years. When she was told the school was bankrupt, she merely stated, "Why are you alarmed? We'll continue." They did and, in 1965, built a facility from scratch on Circular Avenue. It was now called the Paier School of Applied Art and won accreditation as a technical trade school. Thousands of students graduated, and new teachers were brought in, like artist Rudolph Franz Zallinger, who had painted the famous, Pulitzer Prize–winning *Age of Reptiles* mural, reproduced so often in dinosaur books. When Adele died in 1975, Edward decided that rather than quit, he would go even further. He fought for accreditation and finally achieved status as a college with a BFA degree in 198   The Paiers were not the only couple with dreams of academic service. Samuel and Irmagarde Tator had founded the Connecticut College of Commerce in 1929 in New Haven, filling a gap in the area's opportunities for business education. But in 1951, its name was changed to Quinnipiac College in honor of the long-lost tribe. The school moved to Mount Carmel next to the old Jonathan Dickerman farm fifteen years later. Situated along the right arm of the Sleeping Giant, its red-brick architectural unity never failed to impress visiting families or incoming freshmen. Quinnipiac College quickly became a vital part of the Hamden landscape and would continue to reach for greater heights in the decades to come.

That landscape changed thoroughly in the twentieth century as education became more and more essential for success. The last one-room schoolhouse had closed in 1954 in West Woods, and the private Rectory School and Mount Carmel Female Seminary were long gone. However, the tradition of excellence in education remained, and new visionaries tried to advance the town's opportunities. John P. Cushing leased the Pinehurst Mansion on Whitney Avenue and opened Hamden Hall, a private day school for boys in 1912, only the fourth of its kind in the nation. By 1935, it included grades one through twelve and had become a parent-owned, nonprofit, cooperative school. The Eli Whitney Regional Vocational Technical High School, a four-year high school, opened in 1956 to provide students with mastery of various trades and technologies. Following in the footsteps of the Dickerman sisters, Antonine Signorelli founded Sacred Heart Academy as a school for girls, moving to Hamden in 1957. And Hamden High School brought together the community as its creators had hoped, with outstanding curriculum and sports teams. As Julian Schlusberg boasted later in his memoir, *Letters from the Prophets*, the Hamden theatre program won awards for outstanding productions year after year. Of course, they put on Wilder's *Our Town*, "inspired during rehearsals, knowing that his home was literally only blocks away from the school."

Though they lived at the far end of Hamden on Mill Rock, the Wilders chose to be buried here, in the shadow of the Sleeping Giant. *Courtesy of Amy Nawrocki.*

That home became even more important as Thornton aged, his bushy eyebrows turning slowly white. He would entertain guests there, telling stories in front of the big fireplace. From the terrace, he and Isabel could watch the sunset paint the cliffs of East Rock. He invited neighborhood children to play Mozart sonatas with him, put on plays to benefit charities and donated money to promising students at Hamden High School. He enjoyed sampling the local oysters. Whenever he experienced writer's block, he would drive the big Thunderbird up Whitney Avenue to Mount Carmel. "When I get stuck, I can usually work it out by walking up to the tower on Sleeping Giant and down again," he said.

One evening, Isabel woke up and saw that the downstairs lights were on. She passed Thornton's empty bedroom and walked down the staircase, finding him in the living room by the bookshelves, running his hands along the spines of the countless volumes of literature their parents had left them. He looked up at his sister quietly. She asked, "Thornton, is there anything you want?" He answered, "No, I'm just looking—looking for a book that hasn't been written." It was a powerful if unconscious statement on his chosen profession.

At age seventy-six, he finished the ingenious comedy *Theophilus North*, "just a splinter of a much longer" novel. But he would never get the chance to continue it. On December 6, 1975, he stepped through the door of 50 Deepwood Drive and embraced Isabel. "All the way up the wheels said, I'm going home, I'm going home, I'm going home," he told her. The next day, after a light lunch, he died while taking a nap. His own words at the end of *The Bridge of San Luis Rey* seemed an appropriate epitaph: "But soon we will die...and we ourselves shall be loved for a while and forgotten. But the love will have been enough; all those impulses of love return to the love that made them. Even memory is not necessary for love. There is a land of the living and a land of the dead, and the bridge is love. The only survival, the only meaning."

CHAPTER 12

The Poetry of Home

When Donald Hall returned to visit Hamden in the twenty-first century, he was not the same small boy who had lived in Whitneyville and Spring Glen seventy years before. After winning dozens of awards, fellowships and medals, Hall was named the fourteenth United States poet laureate. Though his "returns were memorable," he found the town "altered so much." After seeing his old houses and the site of the Brock-Hall Diary, he visited a friend named Bob McIntosh. Bob had stayed in Hamden and was "riding his bicycle well into his eighties." Perhaps Hall's visit to his old friend showed him that time cannot conquer everything, and with typical Hamden good humor, he tells us, "I walked to school again, wearing knickers over long stockings."

Still, time leaves nothing static, and the new quickly becomes classic. The new Miller Memorial Library and Cultural Center opened in 1980, with sprawling, open-plan architecture that impressed every reader who passes its doors. Five years later, an elderly but spry Isabel Wilder gave permission for the auditorium to be named for her brother and helped plan the replica of his study, donating his desk, chair, lamp and books. Thornton Wilder Hall quickly became the site for plays, debates, town meetings and concerts. Arts and culture seemed to flourish everywhere. Founded by Hank Paper in 1985, Best Video is already an "archive of cinematic history" and consistently rates as the best independent video store in the state. As the new century approached, fine-dining restaurants began to join neighborhood eateries, and now Ibiza offers selections of tasty tapas, Thai Awesome hands out steaming bowls of tom yum soup and Park Central Tavern serves hot plates of Connecticut fried oysters.

Quinnipiac College experienced huge growth at the end of the twentieth century, gaining a law school and becoming a full-fledged university. WQUN was founded by journalist and Professor Lou Adler and became the number one AM station in the area. By 2010, Quinnipiac was offering fifty-two undergraduate majors and twenty graduate programs. Its Polling Institute became nationally recognized and cited, and its sports programs moved to Division I. On nearby York Hill, a new complex sprang up, with basketball and hockey arenas to rival any in the state. Quinnipiac is now a dominant regional university and a strong force in the future of Hamden.

The Mill River Valley knows the tales of Nobel Laureate Sidney Altman, Pulitzer Prize–winning journalist Linda Greenhouse and world-famous theologian Jaroslav Pelikan, all of whom settled down here. There are the stories of world famous "baby doc" Benjamin Spock and actor Dwayne Johnson, who both attended school in town. Many still marvel at the legend of accomplished athlete Scott Burrell, who played three sports at Hamden High, winning the Connecticut High School Basketball Player of Year. In college, Burrell slowed down and played two sports, baseball for the Toronto Blue Jays and basketball for the University of Connecticut, where he became the first player in NCAA history to collect over 1,500 points, 750 rebounds, 275 assists and 300 steals. He was drafted by the Charlotte Hornets and played professional basketball for nine years. The only athlete in major professional sports history to be drafted in the first round in two sports, he returned to his hometown to coach for Quinnipiac University.

There are hundreds of local heroes, like Ken Henrici, who won the Bronze Star in Vietnam, or Bob Bush, killed in action there. Firefighter Ralph Thomaselli was another who put others' lives above his own. This longhaired weightlifter witnessed an explosion in a Whitneyville apartment building in 1977, and after calling his comrades, he rushed into the burning building without equipment to save two people. Police officer Frank McDermott and his dog Hero also made history by saving missing people and helped keep Hamden safe by making hundreds of arrests. Frank founded the K-9 unit in town, and he and Hero were selected as Police Officer of the Year in 2000. Amongst these heroes, we should not forget those who worked to preserve their memories, like Gil Spencer, Dave Johnson or Martha Becker, the sharp-eyed historian who toiled countless hours to save the town's lost stories.

The story of Scott Jackson is already becoming an inspiration to a new generation of Hamden children after he was elected as the town's youngest and first African American mayor in 2009. Scott grew up in Whitneyville, becoming a member of the National Honor Society, as

The Sleeping Giant Fifers drum along Whitney Avenue during the 200th anniversary of the Mount Carmel Congregational Church. *Courtesy of the Mount Carmel Congregational Church.*

well as Hamden High's football and track teams. Working his way up through the town government, he began to "pour a cup of tea, power up my digital camera, and walk," beginning his famous neighborhood tours, which he continued as mayor. "We may have many different neighborhoods, but there is only one Hamden," the lifelong resident pointed out. When he announced his candidacy, he echoed centuries of Hamden pioneers: "You have to dream big."

In these seemingly hasty times, dreams quickly become reality. But although, after three and a half centuries, the Shepherd's Pen has become the site of Hamden Middle School, the past lives on. Eli Whitney's barn, once used for storing and butchering animals, remains intact. Alice Washburn's fabulous colonials still wait around every corner. The Mount Carmel Female Seminary, which had so briefly thrived, is today a beautiful private home. William Linton's *Appledore*, A.C. Gilbert's Mountain View and Thornton Wilder's "house that *The Bridge* built" all still stand. In fact, Hamden is rich with the homes of history: the Amasa Bradley house with its basement tavern, the Elam Ives residence where James grew up and, miraculously, the Ezra Dickerman house, where the three sisters and their brave younger brother spent their fleeting years.

The work of centuries persists as well. The towers of New Haven look like another world from the hill of Hindinger Farm, now a Connecticut Century Farm and on its fourth generation with Hamden's oldest farming family. Even though they are only a mile from the nation's first shopping plaza, Hindinger's potatoes, onions, turnips and rutabagas continue to tempt local taste buds. Over the hill in West Woods, Broken Arrow Nursery's Dick Jaynes has built on his experience with the Connecticut Agricultural Experiment Station to grow and sell fifteen hundred species of plants. Along the way, he became the world's leading expert on Connecticut's state flower, mountain laurel. Down the road from the nursery, Waite Chatterton's 1750 sawmill passed through the Chatterton and Doolittle families until 1984, when it was sold to Craig Reynolds, who worked in the mill as a young man. For 234 years, it operated as "one of the oldest continuously run mills in the country." Though the original equipment was replaced by a circular saw in 1879, Chatterton's mill is still in working order today. Craig still "starts it up" regularly, and you can hear the whirring echoes of the past.

These echoes often become songs of their own. The Eli Whitney Museum has found a home in the old armory and uses hands-on building projects and exhibits to inspire new generations to experiment and invent. The brick and brownstone general store built by James Ives in Mount Carmel became Levine's Market in 1913, and now the Levine grandchildren, the Feinn brothers, run a wine and spirits shop famous for its selection from around the world. Nearby, specialty stores like Bon Appétit and Thyme and Season keep up the market's tradition of bringing quality food to the public. And soon the Rectory Barn, designed by Henry Austin, will find service in the education of children once again.

Nowhere is this song more clearly heard than along the new Farmington Canal Greenway. In 1987, Bob and Ginnie Dowd walked the long canal towpath with mayoral candidate John Carusone. As they picked their way over the railroad ties, they asked him, "If you are elected mayor, are you going to be in favor of this as a walkway?" Though this greenway idea would one day be common, at the time it was a strange one. Nevertheless, Carusone agreed, and Ginnie and Bob were at his office the day after inauguration, leading the fight over the next twenty years to finish the greenway in 2009. One of the Lock keeper's houses on the old canal line has even been restored as a museum and serves as a shelter for the travelers of today.

Perhaps you will be one of those travelers, finding the stories and hidden places of Hamden for yourself. One day you might stop at the ancient Jonathan Dickerman house to explore its modest rooms and primeval herb

A reminder of the never-ending fight for preservation, the old quarry building between the Sleeping Giant and the Mill River disappears slowly into the forest. *Courtesy of the author.*

garden. Crossing the lane that Ezra Day rode to teach Sunday school, you could reflect on the longer path he took to glory and doom. A trail leads along the banks of the Mill River, past the crumbling stone foundation of the Axle Shop and to the site of Munson's ancient dam, where a fly fisherman, the ghost of A.C. Gilbert perhaps, hooks a trout. Taking a fork in the path, you ascend through glacial wreckage to the lip of an old quarry. Below, arches and pillars of a ruin shimmer through the leaves. History itself seems to catch the corner of your eye.

The trail angles up the head of the Sleeping Giant now, and you struggle on steep trap rock, past twisted oaks and cedars. Rising above the blackbird trills, you can see the fading contour of the Farmington Canal, into the soft hills of West Woods and to the northern border at Brooksvale Park. Breathing heavily, legs aching, you pause to watch a peregrine falcon sailing in the updraft. To the south lie Clark's Pond, Spruce Bank and the steeple of the Mount Carmel Congregational Church, where Elizabeth, Abbie and Fannie found their faith. You search the old Cheshire Turnpike for a shadowy hint of Bellamy's Tavern, where the idea of Hamden took shape.

Revolutionary War reenactor Craig Reynolds keeps watch at the Jonathan Dickerman house as the twenty-first century comes to Hamden. *Courtesy of the author.*

At the crest of the slope, the trail leads onto the rugged face of the Giant. A family of deer freezes in the thickets at your approach. Suddenly, the juniper and mountain laurel thins, and you emerge on the jutting chin, near the spot where Arnold Dana fell. You make a slow path along the smoky orange cliffs to the southernmost precipice to sit down and eat a simple lunch of bread and cheese. Past the university, the entire valley unfolds from the ridge of the old Hartford Turnpike. Directly ahead, you can just make out the hollow of Spring Glen, where you might spy an Alice Washburn mansion in the ocean of green.

Beyond, as Donald Hall wrote once about Whitneyville, "the houses lean together for support." There you can find Isabel and Thornton Wilder's small kingdom and the shadowy thwart of East Rock, where William Linton found his peace. And though he is now only a name, once the real Eli Whitney toiled at the far end of this green valley, where today thousands of kindred souls find inspiration. You close your eyes and lean back on the Giant's solid bones, content with your discovery of a good place, worthy of a strong people, a place to create and achieve, to live and love. It might even be a place called home.

Bibliography

Arnold G. Dana Collection. Folders #74, 75, 76, 77, 78, 131. Whitney Library. New Haven Historical Society, New Haven, CT.

Baker, Leigh, Robin Barr, Sarah Benedict and Tasha Eichenseler. *Six Lakes Park: A Vision and Management Plan for the Olin Powder Farm, Hamden, CT*. Yale University School of Forestry and Environmental Studies, May 1, 2004.

Becker, Martha May, and Nancy Davis Sachse. *Hamden: Our Architectural Heritage*. Hamden, CT: Hamden Historical Society, 1986.

Beecher, Mary Jane. *Diary*. 1843. Whitney Library. New Haven Historical Society, New Haven, CT.

Blake, William P. *History of the Town of Hamden, Connecticut*. New Haven, CT: Price, Lee & Co., 1888.

Bryer, Jackson R., ed. *Conversations with Thornton Wilder*. Jackson: University Press of Mississippi, 1992.

Carusone, John L. *The History of Hamden*. Video. Mrs. Ward Becker and Hamden Historical Society, Hamden, CT.

Catalogue of Connecticut Volunteer Organizations with Additional Enlistments and Casualties to July 1864. Hartford, CT: Press of Case, Lockwood and Co., 1864.

Coleman, Mimsie. "The Washburn Touch." *Connecticut Magazine* (March 1990): 71–74.

Collins, Jim. "The Extraordinary Mrs. Washburn." *Yankee Magazine* (May 1991): 103–08.

Craven, Wayne. *Sculpture in America*. New York: Thomas Y. Crowell Company, 1968.

Croffut, W.A., and John M. Morris. *The Military and Civil History of Connecticut During the War of 1861–1865*. Revised 3rd edition. New York: Ledyard Bill, 1869.

Dickerman, Edward Dwight, and George Sherwood Dickerman. *Families of Dickerman Ancestry: Descendants of Thomas Dickerman*. New Haven, CT: Tuttle, Morehouse and Taylor Press, 1897.

Dickerman, George Sherwood. *The Old Mount Carmel Parish: Origins and Outgrowths*. New Haven, CT: Yale University Press for New Haven Colony Historical Society, 1925.

Dickerman, John. H. *Colonial History of the Parish of Mt. Carmel*. New Haven, CT: Press of Ryder's Printing House, 1904.

Elder, Jane Lenz, and David Weber. *Trading in Santa Fe: John M. Kingsbury's Correspondences with James Josiah Webb 1853–1861*. Dallas, TX: Southern Methodist University Press, 1996.

Everest, Winter H. "The Rectory School." *Publications of the Hamden Historical Society*, no. 1. Mount Carmel, CT: Quinnipiack Press, 1938.

Finkelpearl, Tom. "A Trip to Hamden Plaza, or Public Art for the General Public." Art for Public Spaces and Hamden Plaza and David Bermant Foundation, 1987. http://bermant.arts.ucla.edu/press/hamden.htm.

Garre, Kathryn DeFrank. *A Short History of the Growth of an Italian Neighborhood in Hamden, CT 1895–1924*. New Haven: Southern Connecticut State College, 1975.

Gerdts, William. "Chauncey Bradley Ives, American Sculptor." *Antiques* 94, no. 5 (1968).

Gilbert, A.C. *The Man Who Lives in Paradise*. New York: Rinehart and Co., 1954.

Goldberger, Paul, Vincent Scully, Catherine Lynn and Erik Vogt. *Yale in New Haven: Architecture and Urbanism*. New Haven, CT: Yale University, 2004.

Goldstein, Malcolm. *The Art of Thornton Wilder*. Lincoln: University of Nebraska Press, 1965.

Goldstone, Richard. *Thornton Wilder: An Intimate Portrait*. New York: Saturday Review Press, 1975.

Hall, Donald. Letter to Eric D. Lehman, August 3, 2009.

———. *Life Work*. Boston, MA: Beacon Press, 1993.

———. *Old and New Poems*. New York: Ticknor & Fields, 1990.

———. *Unpacking the Boxes*. Boston: Houghton Mifflin Co., 2008.

Hamden Chronicle. "Sleeping Giant Inspiration for Author Thornton Wilder." November 23, 1949.

Hamden Historical Society. *Images of America: Hamden*. Portsmouth, NH: Arcadia Press, 2004.

Hammond, Katheryn N., and Hugh H. Davis. *Historic Hamden: A Guide*. Hamden, CT: Hamden Bicentennial Commission, 1979.

Harrison, Gilbert A. *The Enthusiast: A Life of Thornton Wilder*. New Haven, CT: Ticknor and Fields, 1983.

Hartford Courant. "Ghost Lot Being Exhumed." August 8, 2003.

Hartley, Rachel. *The History of Hamden, Connecticut 1786–1936*. Hamden, CT: Quinnipiack Press, 1943.

Hendrick, Burton J. "William James Linton." *New England Magazine* 28, no. 2 (1898).

Hill, Everett G. *A Modern History of New Haven and Eastern New Haven County*. Vol. I. New York: S.J. Clarke, 1918.

"The History of the Hamden Police Department." Hamden Department of Police Services, 2007. http://www.hamden.com/content.

Johnson, Dave. "Hamden Fire Retirees." Hamden Fire Retirees' Association. http://www.hamdenfireretirees.org.

Linke, Audrey. *World War II Remembered: A Treasury of Heroes*. Hamden, CT, 2005.

Linton, William J. *American Wood Engraving: A Victorian History*. Watkins Glen, NY: The American Life Foundation and Study Institute, 1976.

———. *Memories*. London: Lawrence and Bullen, 1895.

Manual of the Mount Carmel Congregational Church, 1929.

McBride, Florence. *Johnson's Pond in Spring*. Video. 2006.

McCain, Diana Ross. *Connecticut's African-American Soldiers in the Civil War*. Hartford: Connecticut Historical Commission, 2000.

Menta, John. *The Quinnipiac: Cultural Conflict in Southern New England*. New Haven, CT: Yale University Publications in Anthropology, 1535–7082, September 25, 2003.

Mirsky, Jeanette and Allan Nevins. *The World of Eli Whitney*. New York: Macmillan Company, 1952.

MSS#146, Folder K. Whitney Library, New Haven Historical Society, New Haven, CT.

New Haven Register. "Arnold Dana, Economist and Writer, Dies." August 24, 1947.

Newman, Daisy. "Remembering Thornton Wilder." *New York Times*, October 1976.

New York Times. "Farmland: Preserving the Irreplaceable." October 21, 1979.

Niven, John. *Connecticut for the Union*. New Haven, CT: Yale University Press, 1965.

O'Gorman, James F. *Henry Austin*. Middletown, CT: Wesleyan University Press, 2008.

Ralph, A.J. "The Farmington-North Hampton Canal, 1822–1847." *Publications of the Hamden Historical Society*, no. 1. Mount Carmel, CT: Quinnipiack Press. 1938.

Record of Service of Connecticut Men in the Army and Navy of the United States During the War of the Rebellion. Hartford, CT: Press of the Case, Lockwood and Brainard Company, 1889.

Robinson, Ruth Warner. *Chapters from My Childhood on the Old Farm in Mount Carmel, Connecticut, During the Nineteen Teens*. Guilford, CT: Shore Line Times Printing Co, 1970.

Sachse, Nancy Davis. *Born Among the Hills: The Sleeping Giant Story*. 3rd edition. Hamden, CT: Sleeping Giant Association, 1997.

Schlusberg, Julian S. *Letters from the Prophets: A Theater Teacher's Memoir*. New York: Author's Choice Press, 2001.

Schurman, Kathleen. "Reynolds Mill Owner Seeks Historic Recognition." *Hamden Chronicle*, n.d.

Shepard, Janet. *Notes on West Woods*. Hamden, CT: Hamden Historical Society, 1928.

Sills, Charlotte. "The LaFarges: A Connecticut Family of Distinguished Artists." *Connecticut Circle*, May 1938.

Smith, F.B. *Radical Artisan*. Manchester, UK: Manchester University Press, 1973.

Steen, Paula. "Art Is More than a Form at Paier College." *Business Digest*, April 1986, 18–21.

Todd, William. "Chauncey Bradley Ives, Sculptor." *Publications of the Hamden Historical Society*, no. 1. Mount Carmel, CT: Quinnipiack Press. 1938.

———. "Colonel Bellamy and His Tavern." Paper presented to the Hamden Historical Society, October 5, 1939.

———. "William James Linton." *Publications of the Hamden Historical Society*, no. 1. Mount Carmel, CT: Quinnipiack Press, 1938.

Townshend, Charles H. "The Quinnipiack Indians and Their Reservation." *Papers of the New Haven Historical Society* 6. New Haven, CT: Printed for the society, 1900.

Warren, Israel. *The Sisters*. Boston: American Tract Society, 1859.

Watson, Bruce. *The Man Who Changed How Boys and Toys Were Made*. New York: Viking Press, 2002.

Webb, James Josiah. *Adventures in the Sante Fe Trade 1844–1847.* Edited by Ralph Bleber. Lincoln: University of Nebraska Press, 1995.

Welling, William. "Sleeping Giant Inspiration for Author Thornton Wilder." *Hamden Chronicle*, November 23, 1949.

Whitney, Eli. Letter to Ithiel Town, December 26, 1820. MSS #105. Whitney Library. New Haven Historical Society, New Haven, CT.

Wilder, Isabel. Forward. *The Journals of Thornton Wilder 1939–1961.* Edited by Donald Gallup. New Haven, CT: Yale University Press, 1985.

Wilder, Thornton. *The Bridge of San Luis Rey.* New York: Harper Collins Publishers, 2004.

———. *The Journals of Thornton Wilder 1939–1961.* Edited by Donald Gallup. New Haven, CT: Yale University Press, 1985.

Yellig, Martha Finder. *Alice F. Washburn: Architect.* N.p.: Tiger Lily Press, 1990.

About the Author

E ric D. Lehman teaches literature and creative writing at the University of Bridgeport and is the president of the Bridgeport chapter of Phi Kappa Phi. His essays, reviews, poems and stories have been published in dozens of journals and magazines, and his previous book, *Bridgeport: Tales from the Park City*, was released in 2009 by The History Press. Travel writing is his passion, whether he is hiking the Inca Trail in Peru or fly-fishing the rivers of Connecticut. He lives in Hamden with his wife and two cats.

Please visit us at

www.historypress.net